AFRICAN ARK

AFRICAN ARK

PEOPLE AND ANCIENT CULTURES OF ETHIOPIA
AND THE HORN OF AFRICA

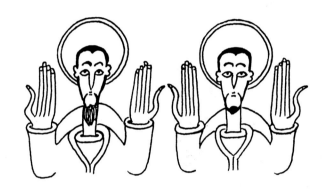

CAROL BECKWITH   ANGELA FISHER

TEXT BY GRAHAM HANCOCK

DESIGN BY BARNEY WAN

HARRY N. ABRAMS, INC., PUBLISHERS, NEW YORK

Other books by the same photographers

Carol Beckwith
NOMADS OF NIGER
MAASAI

Angela Fisher
AFRICA ADORNED

LIBRARY OF CONGRESS CATALOGING-IN-PUBLICATION DATA

Beckwith, Carol.
African ark: people and ancient cultures of Ethiopia and the
Horn of Africa/by Carol Beckwith and Angela Fisher; text by
Graham Hancock.
p.   cm.
Includes bibliographical references.
ISBN 0–8109–1902–8
1. Ethnology—Africa, Northeast.   2. Africa, Northeast—Social
life and customs.   I. Fisher, Angela.   II. Hancock, Graham.
III. Title.
GN650.B43   1990
305.8′0096—dc20   90–30569   CIP

Published in 1990 by Harry N. Abrams, Incorporated, New York

A TIMES MIRROR COMPANY

Printed and bound in West Germany

ACKNOWLEDGMENTS

African Ark was made possible by the generosity of the following organizations and individuals to whom we owe our deepest appreciation:

The Ethiopian Tourism Commission
David H. Koch
Mobil Corporation
The Australian Literary Arts Board

Our book was influenced by the unique culture of Ethiopia and the vision of Comrade Fisseha Geda, the former Commissioner of Tourism. It was he who had seen our previous books on Africa and invited us to consider a similar book on the peoples and cultures of Ethiopia. Our four and a half years of fieldwork fell under his initial guidance and later that of Yohannes Berhanu, Head of Ethiopian Tourism Promotion. The Commission provided us with two extraordinary guides and researchers in the field – Worku Sharew and Zewge Mariam Haile. With their knowledge, devotion and endless patience the difficult task of covering the entire country became not only possible but one of the most unforgettable experiences in our lives. We will treasure their friendship forever.

Under the umbrella of the Ethiopian Tourism Commission we would like to thank the National Tour Operation with a special mention to Yohannes Kifle, Martha Tadesse, and Efrem Teferra, and in the field to NTO staff 'Sargent' Tamru Gabre Wolde, Simone, Gash Mamu, and also to the National Hotel Corporation for assistance in providing accommodation.

To Ethiopian Airlines, we would like to express our gratitude to Captain Mohammed Ahmed, Assefa Tessema, and Kiros Girmay, for their help with airfares and freight during our final year of work. And lastly to Elizabeth Yemane Berhan and Fasil Getachew for assisting us with vital airport formalities.

Due to his many years of devotion to the development of tourism in Ethiopia, Hapte Selassie Taffesse not only supported our project with endless advice, but provided invaluable introductions, insight and hospitality.

This project, initiated and implemented through the good will of the Ethiopian Tourism Commission was further supported by the exceptional generosity of David H. Koch of New York City, and by the enlightened patronage of Mobil Corporation whose general manager in Ethiopia, Jean-Claude Vanson, selected this project as an ongoing cultural contribution to the Ethiopian nation. We would especially like to thank Robert J. McCool, President of Mobil South Inc., and John W. Newlin III, Mobil's Area Executive for Africa. For their generous assistance with our work in Southwest Ethiopia, we would like to thank the National Geographic Society, with special mention to Mary G. Smith, Senior Assistant Editor of Research Grant Projects.

In return for photographic work, the Addis Ababa Hilton Hotel provided accommodation during our short stays in Addis in between field trips during our last year. In particular we would like to thank the following individuals who were especially helpful: Jean Welti, Manager of the Hilton; Lemma Giorgis, Director of Sales; and Abebetch Makonnen, Manager of Public Relations.

There are a number of people in Addis Ababa whose knowledge, friendship and hospitality were not only invaluable but made Ethiopia a home away from home. We would like to extend our special thanks to Marie-France Vanson, Jill and Geoffrey Last, Stella and Alan Bromhead, Irene and Michael Priestley, Barbara and Michael Payson, Titi and Tadesse Zewdie, Helen van Houten, Feleke Ashine, Carlos and Mulu Iori, Conrad Hirsh, Marcello Fanara and John T. Burns.

In Somalia we are most grateful to Yusuf Ali Danab, Ministry of the Interior; Yusuf Abdulai Robleh, Ministry of Information; and Mohamed Abanur (a private citizen); all of whom gave us their time and expertise.

In Djibouti we would like to thank Moussa Robleh, Director of Djibouti Tourism Bureau, and Lefty Repapis, Manager of the Sheraton Hotel, for their willingness to help in every way.

For assistance and hospitality during our many field expeditions we would like to thank the following: – in Lalibela: Aba Berhane Selassie, the Bishop of Lasta: Kes Yitabarak; Dr Richard Pankhurst; and World Vision. In Gondar: Ahmed Beshir, Regional Director of NTO, and Yewbnker Yehalashet of Woleka. In Eritrea: Abraham Ghebre-Egzi, ETC Rep for Eritrea Region; Eyob Ocbayesus, R.R.C. Manager; Mohammed Ahmed, Beni Amer Chief; Baharu Alema, Red Sea Hotel Manager; Ali Eidahiz, Chairman of the Farmers' Association Asaita. In Djibouti: Abdoul Kader Houmed, Sultan of Tadjourah, Ali 'no-time-to-lose', our indefatigable and charming guide and driver from the Tourist Bureau. In Somalia: Sarah Saeed; the family of Mohammed Abanur in Brava with special thanks to Khadijah and Aba; and Carol Yot who gave much of her time co-ordinating our itinerary from England. In Kenya: Ahmed Sheikh Badawy, Education Officer, Lamu Museum; and Dr Linda Donley-Reid, research fellow, U. of C. Berkeley, California. In Southwest Ethiopia, for the Konso: Dinote Kusia Shenkere, researcher and guide. For the Hamar: Makonnen Dori, Ivo Strecker, and Father Brian O'Toole of the Dimeka Catholic Mission – top authorities on Hamar; Okoda Boya, guide and translator; and Chief Hailu. For the Surma: Feleke Balcha, translator; Bikaden, guide and translator; Chief Doleti and Chief Bedumba; Kolaholi, Chinoi and Muradit – Surma friends and assistants. For the Karo: Amerikan, Acha, Doray and Kawo – Karo guides and friends.

Of the very few travelling companions we had, we would like to thank David Coulson who contributed the photograph on pages 62 and 63, Lee Harvin, Ira Cohen and Balcha Gebretsadik for their good will, friendship and great help on route.

For the production of *African Ark* we would like to give special thanks to Christopher MacLehose our publisher at Collins Harvill who has once again been a pillar of support, having sustained belief in our project from its inception. We would also like to thank Robert Morton and Paul Gottleib from Harry N. Abrams for their commitment and invaluable partnership, and Toby Eady, our agent, for his great talent in assuring the smooth flow of a complex production.

At Collins, Ron Clark, director of the Art Department, has overseen our project with characteristic care and calm sensitivity. Meanwhile, Bill Swainson, text editor, Heather Wardle, production manager, and Marco Tomasi of fotolito CLG, Verona, have put in endless hours of dedicated work.

For assistance with final picture selection, we would like to thank Yorick Blumenfeld, Robert Freeman, Steve Lovi, Eve Arnold, Mirella Ricciardi, Hansjorg Mayer, Mimi Lipton and Maria Alexander; for his creative touch in designing maps, Stephen Raw; and for reading text, Amy and Louise Godine.

Graham Hancock, the author of the text, has spent fifteen years living and working in the horn of Africa and has written five books on social and cultural issues of Ethiopia, Somalia and Djibouti. We invited Graham to write the text because of his extensive knowledge and love of the region. His exceptional cooperation and willingness made him a pleasure both to work and travel with. His assistance in organizing our fieldwork in Somalia and Djibouti was invaluable.

The two of us combined as photographers with the hope of making a book on Africa that would be more outstanding than any of our previous solo efforts. Such a goal would only have been possible with the support of the right designer. Barney Wan was that singular person who enabled us to produce the book we dreamed of. His approach to design is not only truly creative but took into account all our concepts and sensitivities throughout the ten month period from picture editing to final layouts. For us he has proved to be the perfect designer. His creative contribution was equalled by his devoted friendship, not to mention his wonderful cooking.

And lastly for the continued support and love of our families, we would like to thank Leo and Marylyn Beckwith, and Simon and Kate Fisher.

C.B. and A.F.

Bishop of Lasta at Lalibela

Afar woman of Tadjourah

CHAPTER

1

PRAYERS
OF
STONE

13

Church painting from Gondar

Somali camel herder

CHAPTER

2

THE
HEAVENLY
WORLD

49

Rashaida woman of Eritrea

Sheikh Hussein pilgrim

CHAPTER

3

THE DESERT
AT THE
MOUNTAINS' FEET

77

CHAPTER

4

EMPIRE OF
THE SENSES

119

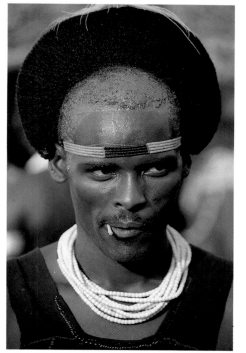

Hamar initiate into manhood

CHAPTER

7

PEOPLES
OF THE
MORNING

205

CHAPTER

5

GAUNT AND
LEOPARD-COLOURED
LANDS

145

Chalk-painted Surma girls

CHAPTER

8

PEOPLES
OF THE
WILDERNESS

249

CHAPTER

6

SPIRIT
WORLDS

175

Karo girl from the Omo river

CHAPTER

9

EPITAPH
TO AN
IDEA

299

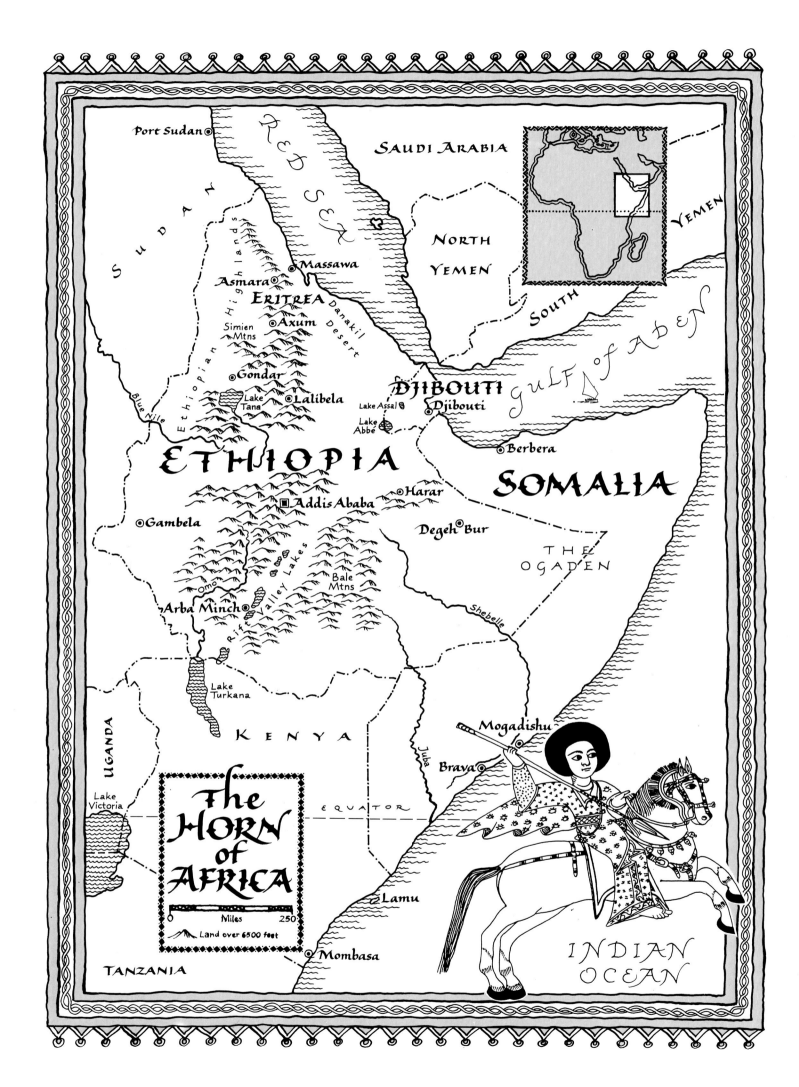

Port Sudan

SAUDI ARABIA

RED SEA

NORTH YEMEN

YEMEN

SOUTH

GULF OF ADEN

Massawa

Asmara

ERITREA

Danakil Desert

Simien Mtns

Axum

Ethiopian Highlands

Gondar

DJIBOUTI

Djibouti

Lake Tana

Lalibela

Lake Assal

Lake Abbé

Berbera

Blue Nile

ETHIOPIA

SOMALIA

Harar

Addis Ababa

Gambela

Degeh Bur

THE OGADEN

Arba Minch

Omo

Bale Mtns

Shebelle

Rift Valley Lakes

Lake Turkana

KENYA

Juba

Mogadishu

Brava

Lake Victoria

UGANDA

The HORN of AFRICA

EQUATOR

Lamu

0   Miles   250

Land over 6500 feet

INDIAN OCEAN

Mombasa

TANZANIA

PREFACE

The Horn of Africa has drawn us to it for nearly two decades, exerting a special magnetism that has brought us back again and again. Maybe this attraction stems from the fact that much of the Horn is wild in a way that few parts of Africa can claim to be, and thus still free in spirit. It has this quality partly because the colonial era left almost no mark here, but also because of the fiercely independent character of the Ethiopian and Somali people who make up most of the sixty million inhabitants. Cut off from the wider world by soaring mountain ranges, burning lava deserts, trackless expanses of wilderness, and an isolated Indian Ocean coastline battered by the southwest monsoons, the ancient cultures of the region have retained their vigour and diversity unadulterated by Western influences. In the end we decided that it was our love of these cultures, more than anything else, that kept calling us back.

The three of us – two photographers and a writer – met for the first time in Addis Ababa in 1984, and it was at that initial meeting that this book began to take shape. Five years of fieldwork followed in Ethiopia, Djibouti, and Somalia, and also in adjoining parts of Northern Kenya and of the Eastern Sudan. As we photographed and researched in these countries, we could not help but be involved in the truly momentous events that were going on all around us. The famines, wars and epidemics to which the Horn of Africa has been subject in the last decade often made it difficult to hold the focus on our chosen subject.

The famine of 1984–85, which focused the world's attention on the Horn, was indeed a terrible event, and its consequences are still being felt. For us, it was the worst experience of human suffering we had ever known. To put it into historical perspective, however, the peoples of this region have survived more than forty recorded famines since the ninth century, many of far greater severity than the disasters covered by television. In the Great Famine of 1888–92, for instance, more than two-thirds of the entire population of Ethiopia died; in the years 1435–36, an epidemic raged that "destroyed the inhabitants of Abyssinia"; earlier still a tenth-century Christian Emperor of Ethiopia wrote the following in a letter to the Patriarch of Alexandria: "Great tribulation hath come upon our land and all our men are dying of the plague, and our beasts and cattle have perished, and God hath restrained the heavens so that they cannot rain . . ."[1]

As with famine, so also with war. The civil and secessionist conflicts, rebellions, invasions and revolutions which the Horn has endured in the twentieth century are the successors to those of times gone by – Ethiopia has hardly known a single decade of unbroken peace since proper records were started more than seven hundred years ago. In the sixteenth century, to take but one example, the Somali commander Ahmed Gragn invaded Abyssinia. In this war of cross and crescent, tens of thousands of people were killed, churches were burnt down, and towns and villages were razed across the length and breadth of the land.

Although hunger and fighting are part of the story, the really remarkable feature of this region is surely its triumphant spirit of endurance, its unquenchable life force. This book is a quest for that life force, a journey without maps through a region that belongs to no single nation or people and that is, in truth, more an idea than a place.

Vast and remote, the Horn of Africa is an Ark that shelters an astonishing variety of human societies: from the ancient and highly sophisticated to the remote, simple and untouched, from mountain dwellers to desert nomads, from sea traders to river fishermen, from hunters to artists – all of whom have their place in this microcosm of the African continent.

In trying to capture the spirit of this extraordinary region we hope that we have made some contribution towards preserving it. Our planet would be vastly poorer if the terrible pressures which the Horn is now suffering were allowed to triumph over the creative resiliance of its peoples. If that were to happen something vital and precious would have been taken away forever from the sum of mankind's experience.

CAROL BECKWITH, ANGELA FISHER, GRAHAM HANCOCK
LONDON, JANUARY 1990

INTRODUCTION

Despite their marked differences, the many tribes and "nations" into which the sixty million inhabitants of the Horn of Africa are divided *all* belong to just two great ethnic groups – the Semitic and Hamitic families.*

According to the Biblical account, Noah's sons Ham and Shem fathered the Hamitic and Semitic lines after they stepped out from the Ark. It is thus fitting, in the Horn of Africa today that their descendants continue to be inspired by ancient faiths to which they adhere with an unshakable devotion. Judaism came to the Horn in the epoch of Solomon; in the chilly mountain fastnesses of northern Ethiopia it is still practised in its authentic pre-Talmudic form. Likewise, archaic Christianity – dating back at least to the fourth century AD – exerts a powerful influence on the lives of millions. Islam, too, brought here during the lifetime of the Prophet Mohammed, flourishes across vast areas. Last but not least, ancestor worship and a reverence for spirits of the bush survive in many isolated pockets and in many forms.

According to Ethiopian legend, the Holy Ark of the Covenant was brought from Jerusalem to Axum by Menelik, son of King Solomon and the Queen of Sheba.

Sacred preoccupations are inextricably bound up with everyday pursuits in almost all the Horn's diverse societies. In the mountain regions, settled agriculture on tidy, regular fields is the dominant lifestyle. Though the horizons of the villagers seem to extend no further than the peak that looms above, the valley that plunges below, they are nevertheless a people engaged in unbroken communion with the infinite: no traveller who has attended services in their synagogues and churches, or joined them on a pilgrimage, could doubt this for a moment. On the open rangelands, pastoral nomads jealously guard their cattle and water rights; though they bow to no man, they prostrate themselves five times a day before the unfathomable will of Allah. On the southern plains, possibly the last hunter-gatherers that Africa will ever know raid the land for its bounty as their fathers and their fathers' fathers did before them: in rocks and stones, in caves, trees and running water they, too, find something divine and worthy of worship.

Just as people express ideas that are central to their civilization through the passion with which they adhere to their faith, so also they give shape to the notions that they hold about themselves through their artforms. In these respects the preoccupations of settled farmers are inevitably different from those of their nomadic cousins. It is thus hardly surprising, in the highlands of the Horn of Africa, which have been intensively cultivated for at least three millennia, that the dominant art forms should be carvings, architecture, paintings: all things that require time, patience, and the passing of many seasons to bring to fruition. Down on the plains, by contrast, where pastoralism holds sway, everything seems to be written in sand – there are few artifacts and few posses-

---

* These ethnic groups are most clearly defined by the languages they speak. Thus, highland Ethiopians who speak Amharic – a language related to both Arabic and Hebrew – are classified by ethnologists as a Semitic people. By contrast, the Somalis speak a Hamitic language that bears no structural resemblance to Amharic (or to Arabic or Hebrew either). Somali is closely related to the Oromo and Afar tongues spoken by neighbouring Hamitic peoples living within the borders of Ethiopia.

sions; portability and convenience are paramount. Yet, among the hardbitten and preliterate nomads of these desert lands has flowered the most exquisite oral poetry:

> A fleeting vision suddenly appeared
> Her colour like a lighted lantern.
> In sleep she comes to lie with me
> And early in the dawn she leaves
> As in a whirling shaft of dust
> Driven by the wind.[1]

Some of the peoples of the Horn of Africa have been in close contact with the outside world for centuries – notably the coastal communities linked through the dhow trade with Arabia, India and China. Here art, music, jewellery and architecture all reflect a refined cosmopolitanism, an acceptance and absorption of the best that is available from alien cultures. Other more isolated groups, equipped with only the crudest tools and materials, have sought to make the most of the one canvas that is reliably available to them – the human form itself. Scarification and elaborate body painting express the animus of such peoples to no greater or lesser extent than the spirit of the Renaissance is expressed by Michelangelo's "David".

Our journey, intended as an exploration and celebration of all these different cultures, begins in the highlands of Abyssinia amid the ancient Christian ceremonies that take place each year in the rock-hewn churches of Lalibela. We then move north to Axum, the birthplace of Ethiopian Christianity in the fourth century AD and a city which many believe to have been the home of the Queen of Sheba.

Chapter Two introduces the Falashas, a disappearing tribe of Ethiopian Jews whose origins are lost in the mists of history. Living around Lake Tana and in the mountainous terrain to the north of the fortress city of Gondar, they are surrounded on all sides by the dominant Amharas – a Christian Semitic people who have had a powerful influence on Abyssinia's artistic and material culture. The churches of Gondar and the monasteries on the islands of Lake Tana are repositories of Christian art which protect centuries of priceless religious treasures.

Chapter Three brings an abrupt change of emphasis. Moving down out of the highlands into the low-lying deserts of the Great Rift Valley, it explores the hard pastoral life of the Afar and the Beja – Hamitic clans renowned for their cruelty, warrior valour and uncompromising independence of spirit. In the last one hundred and fifty years these clans have been joined by Bedouin nomads known as the Rashaida, who migrated across the Red Sea from Saudi Arabia.

In Chapter Four the pace changes again, echoing the gentler rhythms of the Horn's long seaboard – which extends from the Red Sea port of Massawa to the Indian Ocean island of Lamu. For centuries the dhow sea trade has connected the coastal settlements to Arabia, India and the Far East, bringing religion, knowledge, inspiration and wealth from these faraway places.

By contrast an entirely different ethic dominates the gaunt and leopard-coloured lands of the Horn's interior. Here Somali nomads, who own almost one half of the world's camel population, follow their herds from one transitory pasture to the next, just as their ancestors did for countless generations before them. Like the Afar and the Beja, to whom they are related, they obey the laws of Patriarchal times – an eye for an eye, a tooth for a tooth, and 100 camels for the life of a man.

Chapter Six moves deeper inland to the remote foothills of the Bale mountains in southeastern Ethiopia. In this region, as yet only lightly brushed by the Islamic faith that holds sway among the nomads and on the coast, a strange ecstatic religion has evolved. Part Muslim and part spirit cult, it draws tens of thousands of enraptured pilgrims every year to the sacred shrines of long-dead holy men.

Chapters Seven, Eight and Nine bring us to the far southwest of the Horn among peoples who have only recently made any contact at all with the outside world. Pastoralists, hunter-gatherers and farmers, they live in close contact with nature, revering the power of their ancestors and the spirits of the bush. Their ancient customs include initiation ceremonies and stick fighting, body painting and scarification, and the wearing of lip plates. Theirs are some of the last few traditional societies remaining in Africa today. It is with a recognition of their vulnerability in the face of recent and rapid change that our journey and celebration ends.

CHAPTER ONE

PRAYERS OF STONE

The Christian Highlands: Lalibela and Axum

"Encompassed by the enemies of their religion, the Ethiopians slept for near a thousand years, forgetful of the world by whom they were forgotten . . ." Edward Gibbon's eloquent comment refers roughly to the period from the seventh to the sixteenth centuries AD. He perhaps overstates the world's forgetfulness: isolated by giant mountains, Abyssinia was thought of by many in medieval Europe as a place of compelling mystery – the fabulous realm of Prester John. During the Crusades, it came to exert a special magnetism: as the only Christian kingdom in Africa or Asia it was regarded as a potentially powerful ally against Islam.

The Ethiopians themselves, however, were very much on the defensive. Despite the Prophet Mohammed's seventh-century injunction to his followers to "leave the Abyssinians in peace", Muslim invaders did subsequently attack and occupy much of the Horn's northern coastal zone. In so doing they rolled back the frontiers of what had once been the most important secular power between the Roman Empire and Persia – a power that, in days gone by, had sent its navies sailing across the seas to Egypt, India, Celyon and China.

Lamenting their lost grandeur, Ethiopia's rulers retreated with their Christian subjects into the remote central uplands of their vast country. There, protected by formidable mountain battlements, they were able to resist further intrusions – trapping their enemies in the labyrinth of valleys intersecting the high plateau.

A fortress mentality took root during these centuries of retreat. Indeed, in keeping out the hated "enemies of their religion" the Ethiopians also cut themselves off from the evolving mainstream of Christian thought. It was in this sense alone that they "slept". Otherwise, the civilization of the highlands was very much awake.

Many of the improvizations of these times were so vital that they have endured to the present day as living expressions of the central and lasting values of Christian Ethiopian culture. Foremost amongst these priceless legacies is the monastic settlement of Lalibela which stands at an altitude of some 8,500 feet on a natural rock terrace in the north of the province of Wollo.

LEFT: Deacon with processional cross during *Genna* (Christmas) celebrations.

A selection of silver neck pendants from different regions of the Ethiopian highlands. From top to bottom: Lalibela cross, Welega cross, and Falasha Star of David.

A CITY CARVED FROM LEGEND

Once the thriving capital city of a medieval dynasty, Lalibela has been reduced by the passing centuries to the proportions of a village. Approached by road from below, it is for a long while invisible against a horizon dominated by the towering peak of Mount Abune Yosef. Even from quite close up it seems unremarkable. Yet it is precisely to this camouflaged, chameleon quality that Lalibela owes its longevity. Here, some eight hundred years ago, safe from prying eyes and plundering armies, a secret marvel was fashioned – a marvel considered by many to be the eighth wonder of the world.

According to legend a prince was born in Roha (the old name for Lalibela) in the second half of the twelfth century. He was the youngest son of the royal line of the Zagwe dynasty which then ruled over much of northern Ethiopia. Not long after his birth, his mother saw a dense swarm of bees surrounding him in his crib and, recalling an old belief that the animal world could foretell the future of important personages, she cried out "Lalibela" – meaning, literally, "the bees recognize his sovereignty".

The boy was christened and as he grew so did the jealousy of the reigning monarch, who eventually poisoned him. While his life hung in the balance, God took him up to heaven and there revealed His great purpose: Lalibela would survive, and would become King; in return, however, he was to build eleven churches, the like of which the world had never seen before. These churches were to follow a masterplan which the Almighty then revealed.

As soon as he had ascended the throne, Lalibela set about fulfilling the task that had been set him. The story has it that angels joined the labourers by day and continued the work at night, thus ensuring exact and speedy compliance with the Lord's command.

CHURCHES IN ROCK

Towering edifices, the Lalibela churches were not *built* at all in the conventional sense. Instead they were hewn directly out of the solid red volcanic rock on which they stand. Close examination is required before the full extent of this achievement can be appreciated: some of the churches lie almost completely concealed within deep trenches, while others hide in the open mouths of quarried caves. Connecting them all is a complicated network of tunnels and narrow passageways with offset crypts, grottos and galleries – a cool, lichen-enshrouded, subterranean world, shaded and damp, silent but for the faint echoes of distant footfalls as priests and deacons go about their timeless business.

Four of the Lalibela churches are completely freestanding, being attached to the surrounding rock only by their bases. These are Beta Medhane Alem (the House of the Saviour of the World), Beta Mariam (the House of Mary), Beta Amanuel (the House of Emanuel) and Beta Ghiorghis (the House of St George). Although their individual dimensions and configurations are very different, all four take the form of great blocks of stone, precisely sculptured to resemble normal buildings yet completely isolated within the deep courtyards excavated around them.

In addition, there are seven other rock-hewn churches in Lalibela. These, although not strictly speaking "monolithic", demonstrate various degrees of separation from the surrounding volcanic tuff. Beta Abba Libanos, for example is "semi-detached": all four of its walls are isolated but its roof merges into the cliff above. By contrast, Beta Golgotha (the House of Golgotha) and Beta Qedus Mikael (the House of St Michael) are both much more completely subterranean – although the latter has three exposed facades and the former has one.

Setting aside the legendary interventions of supernatural beings, how exactly were Lalibela's wonders created? Today we can only guess: the techniques that made possible the excavation and chiselling of stone on so dramatic a scale, and with such perfection, have long been lost. Nevertheless, this was, undoubtedly, a human achievement and also a peculiarly *Ethiopian* achievement: our world contains nothing else quite like the rock-hewn churches.

The architects who carried out the King's commission, though certainly not angels, must have been both skilled and knowledgeable. It is nevertheless highly improbable that their labours were completed in just twenty-four years – as the legends insist. Probably the work went on long after Lalibela's death – indeed, his queen, Maskal Kabra, is acknowledged to have built Beta Abba Libanos in his memory (with the help of angels, of course, and in just one night).

The first European to visit Lalibela was a Portuguese friar, Francisco Alvarez, who arrived in the 1520s on an expedition to convert the Coptic Abyssinians to Roman Catholicism. He was overwhelmed by what he found in this remote mountain stronghold – perhaps because it so completely contradicted his notions of European cultural superiority – and he became convinced that his peers would not believe his account. After describing all the churches in turn, he therefore concluded: "I swear by God, in whose power I am, that all that is written is the truth, and there is much more than I have already written, and I have left it that they may not tax me with its being falsehood."

A LIVING FAITH

The Lalibela churches testify to the power and spirit of the archaic Christian faith – a faith that, at the end of the second millennium, retains its hold on hearts and minds in the Ethiopian north with an undiminished vigour. Here, throughout the year, worshippers come to celebrate the shared values of their widely scattered highland communities.

The most heavily attended services are those that occur at dawn, before the arduous work in the fields begins. Participating in the ceremonies in the chill grey light, one has the sense of leaving the modern age behind: the ponderous, rhythmical music with its undertone of drums and tambourines, the aspiring chant of the deacons, members of the congregation giving thanks or calling out for the mercy of God, the cold dark walls, the rough stone floor, the silhouettes of people standing, leaning on prayer sticks, or slumped down in obeisance – all these sights, sounds and sensations seem to constitute an unbroken link with another time. It becomes easy to understand how powerful the call of original Christianity must have been – how it inspired the imagination of millions and spread like wildfire across vast areas of the known world. This was the Church that performed miracles, healed the sick, raised the dead: in this context the feeding of the five thousand, the story of Lazarus, Christ walking on the water, all appear to be perfectly comprehensible. Indeed, among those who come to Lalibela's rock-hewn churches, miracles are still unquestioningly believed to stem from the pure energy of faith focussed through the lives of saints and holy men, and the words of the Bible are seen as nothing less than revealed truths which no one may question.

At *Genna* (Christmas) – which, according to Ethiopia's Julian Calendar,[1] takes place not in December but in early January – and at *Timkat* (Epiphany), which is celebrated twelve days later, Lalibela's role as a place of active worship becomes particularly clear. Then, even in the hardest of times, tens of thousands of pilgrims gather. Many walk for days, months even, from far-off hamlets in inaccessible valleys, to be here at this season: the old and the young, the healthy and the sick, the barren and the fruitful – all come at their own pace to participate in the ceremonies of worship.

The *Timkat* rituals commemorate St John's baptism of Christ in the waters of the River Jordan. Lalibela, too, has a river of this name – which features prominently in the ceremonies (even though successive droughts mean that it has been dry for some years).

Each year the same pattern is repeated. First, on 18 January – *Ketera*, the eve of Epiphany – the holy *tabots* of the rock-hewn churches are brought out in procession and carried to the banks of the Jordan. These engraved slabs of stone or wood represent the Tables of the Law that, in Old Testament times, were supposedly conveyed to Ethiopia

Neck pendants. From top to bottom: lion's claw, ear pick, glass talisman and Gojjam cross.

15

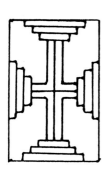

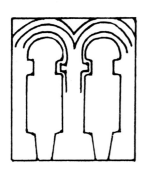

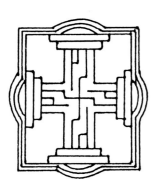

Carved windows from the rock churches of Lalibela. From top to bottom: Bete Ghiorghis, Bete Mariam, and Bete Mikael (last two).

in the Ark of the Covenant; they also embody the intangible notion of sanctity.

The *tabots* are regarded with extreme reverence, for it is they, rather than the churches that house them, that are consecrated; indeed, without a *tabot* at its heart, in its holy of holies, a church is just an empty husk – a dead building of no greater or lesser significance than any other. For this reason, shielded from the profane gaze of the laity, the *tabots* are wrapped in richly embroidered silks and fine gold and silver brocades whenever they are brought into a public place. At Lalibela they are borne down to the banks of the Jordan on the turbanned heads of senior priests who, in their turn, are preceded by younger deacons wearing filigree crowns and carrying ornate crosses; meanwhile, others in the procession hold aloft multicoloured ceremonial umbrellas representative of the celestial spheres. The ringing of hand bells, the jingle of sistra and the blowing of trumpets add wild, evocative sounds to the spectacle, and the fragrance of frankincense and myrrh distributed from swinging bronze censors fills the evening air.

The *tabots* are installed in a specially erected tent overnight while the priests keep up a long vigil of prayer. Then, around dawn, mass and communion are held, after which the baptismal ceremonies of Epiphany proper begin. In this fashion, amid great poverty but with undiminished conviction, the two-thousand-year-old rite of baptism continues to be conducted in Ethiopia today.

When all is done, the crowds wind their way back from the valley of the Jordan towards the stone churches of Lalibela. To these churches now, wrapped in their worn but still lustrous brocades, the *tabots* are also returned – borne as before on the heads of the elders in a procession enlivened by the singing and dancing of the younger priests, and the music of sistra, drums and trumpets. Thus, perhaps, as the Bible states, did "David and all the House of Israel play before the Lord on all manner of instruments, made of fir wood, even on harps and on psalteries, and on timbrels, and on cornets, and on symbals. . . ."[2]

THE QUEEN OF SHEBA

The first written records pertaining to the Horn of Africa date back approximately four thousand five hundred years. We owe these early historical commentaries to two of the very first centres of human civilization, Persia and Egypt – for both of which the Horn seems to have served as an emporium of much-prized tropical products. Egyptian hieroglyphic records indicate that the Pharaohs obtained frankincense and myrrh from Ethiopia, and from the Somali coast, as far back as 2700 BC. Trade with India was likewise of great antiquity – the Horn has supplied the subcontinent with vast quantities of ivory since time immemorial.

It was ancient contacts such as these that nurtured and strengthened the emerging culture of the peoples of northern Ethiopia. The result – not long after David's reign in Israel – was the establishment of a kingdom that was to dominate the vital crossroads of Africa and Asia for more than a thousand years. Conducting its foreign trade through the Red Sea port of Adulis, this kingdom's capital was Axum – described by Nonnosus, Ambassador of the Roman Emperor Justinian, as "the greatest city of all Ethiopia".

Today silent witness is borne to this noble past by extensive ruins of temples, fortresses and palaces as well as by a series of vast *stelae* – carved granite monoliths, some of which exceed 65 feet in height and weigh more than 500 tons. Adding substance to chimeras and testifying to the lost truths embedded in myths and fables, the bones of long-gone eras protrude everywhere through the soil and hordes of gold, silver and bronze coins continue to be washed out from time to time by heavy downpours of rain.

Axum's greatest significance, however, is not as an archaeological site but rather as the supposed capital of the Queen of Sheba – the capital from whence she set out on her legendary visit to the court of Solomon in Jerusalem. Upon this story, with some unusual embellishments, rests the notion of the sacral kingship of the Semitic peoples of Ethiopia – a notion that links the recent past to ancient times in a most unambiguous fashion. Emperor Haile Selassie was, after all, the 225th monarch of a dynasty that traced its descent back to the union of Solomon and Sheba. The revolution of 1974, and the Emperor's death in obscure circumstances a year later, thus marked the end of an immense era – and the beginning of the end for an entire way of life and an entire system of values associated with it.

The legend of Solomon and Sheba is one of great mythopoeic power that has infiltrated numerous cultures outside Ethiopia. The earliest known version is preserved in two books of the Old Testament. Here we are told that the Queen of Sheba, lured by Solomon's fame, journeyed to Jerusalem with a great caravan of costly presents and there "communed with him of all that was in her heart". King Solomon, for his part, "gave to the Queen of Sheba all her desire . . . So she turned and went to her own land, she and her servants." The Talmud also contains oblique references to the story, as does the New Testament (where Sheba is referred to as "the Queen of the South"). There is, in addition, a fairly detailed account in the Koran, echoed in several Arabic and Persian folk tales of later date (in which she is known as *Bilqis*). Further afield, in southern Africa, the enigmatic stone ruins of Great Zimbabwe are said by the local Mashona people to have been the palace of the Queen of Sheba, and tribal elders still repeat their own fully evolved version of the legend. Of all these different narratives, however, it is the Ethiopian variant (where Sheba's name becomes *Makeda*) that is the richest and the most convincing – despite the fact that it does not seem to have been set down in writing until medieval times when it appeared in the *Kebra Nagast* (Glory of Kings), the Ethiopian national saga.

One thing is certain: the veneration of the Queen of Sheba – and her appropriation as the spiritual ancestress of the Ethiopian people – began much earlier than the fourteenth century (when the *Kebra Nagast* was written); indeed, the cult of Makeda probably substantially predates the Christian era.[3] As a historical figure she is thought to have lived in the period between 1000 and 950 BC and, despite a rival claim from South Arabia, the evidence is extremely strong that her capital was indeed in Abyssinia – although not necessarily in the city of Axum.

It is in Axum, however, that the Ethiopians locate her. From here, according to the *Kebra Nagast*, she was persuaded to travel to the court of Solomon by the head of her caravans – a man much impressed by the King's wisdom and might. In Jerusalem a banquet of specially seasoned meat was given in her honour and, at the end of the evening, Solomon invited her to spend the night in his chambers. Makeda agreed, but first extracted a commitment from the King that he would not take her by force. To this he assented, on the single condition that the Queen make a promise not to take anything in his house. Solomon then mounted his bed on one side of the chamber and had the Queen's bed prepared at the other side, placing near it a bowl of water. Made thirsty by the seasoned food, Makeda soon awoke, arose, and drank the water. At this point Solomon seized her hand and accused her of having broken her oath; he then "worked his will with her".

That night the King dreamt that a brilliant light, the divine presence, had left Israel. Shortly afterwards the Queen departed and returned to her country and there, nine months and five days later, she gave birth to a son – Menelik, the founder of Ethiopia's Solomonic dynasty.

In due course, when the boy had grown, he went to visit his father who received him with great honour and splendour. After spending a year at court in Jerusalem, however, the prince determined to return once more to Ethiopia. When he was informed of this, Solomon assembled the elders of Israel and commanded them to send their firstborn sons with Menelik. Before the young men departed, however, they stole the Ark of the Covenant and took it with them to Ethiopia – which then, according to the *Kebra Nagast*, became "the second Zion".

The notion that the Ark of the Covenant was removed from Jerusalem to Axum is central to the reverence accorded to the *tabots*, the Tablets of the Law, in Abyssinian

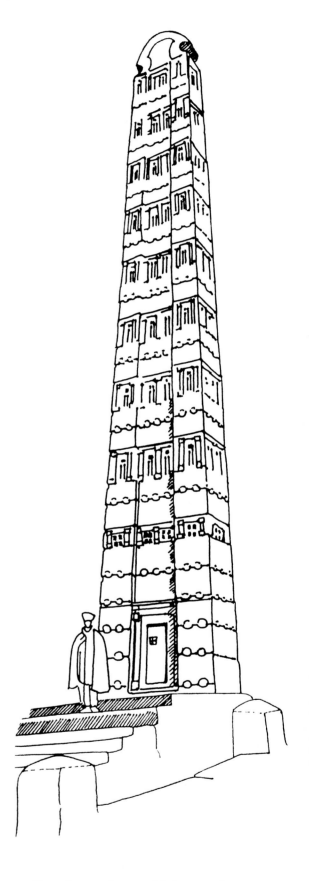

Two-thousand-year-old Axum *stele* standing 75 feet high.

Christian practices. The belief system of which the *tabots* are a part is, however, an unusual one. No other Christian Church gives such importance to what is, by definition, a pre-Christian – indeed a Judaic – tradition. Furthermore, the Christian faith did not itself reach Ethiopia until the fourth century AD – some one thousand three hundred years after Solomon's rule in Israel. The only satisfactory explanation for the unique position given to the Ark and to the *tabots*, therefore, is this: in Old Testament times, there must have been a period when there were very close cultural and religious links between Abyssinia and the Holy Land. Could it not be that the Queen of Sheba "legend" and the story of Menelik bear witness to this deeper truth?

This is a matter on which there may never be any final or incontrovertible proof. What is beyond dispute, however, is that the Axumite realm converted to Christianity in the fourth century AD during the reign of King Ezana, who thus occupies a vitally important place in Ethiopian history.

The story of the conversion, which has its roots in the reign of Ezana's father, King Ella Amida, is preserved in the writings of the fourth-century Byzantine theologian Rufinius. He records that a certain Meropius, a Christian merchant, or – as he calls him – a "philosopher of Tyre", once made a voyage to India, taking with him two Syrian boys whom he was educating in "humane studies". The elder was called Frumentius and the younger Aedesius. On their return journey through the Red Sea, the ship was seized off the African coast, apparently as a reprisal against the Eastern Roman Empire which had broken a treaty with the people of the area.

Meropius was killed in the fighting. The boys, however, survived and were taken to the Axumite King, Ella Amida, who promptly made Aedesius his cupbearer and Frumentius, the more sagacious and prudent of the two, his treasurer and secretary. Rufinius states that the two boys were held in great honour and affection by the King who, however, died shortly afterwards leaving his widow and an infant son, Ezana, as his heir. Before his death, Ella Amida had given the two Syrians their freedom but the Queen begged them, with tears in her eyes, to stay with her until her son came of age. She asked in particular for the help of Frumentius – for Aedesius, though loyal and honest at heart, was simple.

During the years that followed, the influence of Frumentius in the Axumite kingdom grew. He is said to have sought out such foreign traders who were Christians and urged them "to establish conventicles in various places to which they might resort for prayer". He also provided them with "whatever was needed, supplying sites for buildings and in every way promoting the growth of the seed of Christianity in the country".

At around the time that Ezana finally ascended the throne, Aedesius returned to Tyre. Frumentius for his part journeyed to Alexandria, then a great centre of Christianity, where he informed Patriarch Athanasius of the work so far accomplished for the faith in Ethiopia. The young man begged the ecclesiastical leader "to look for some worthy man to send as bishop over the many Christians already congregated". Athanasius, having carefully weighed and considered the words of Frumentius, declared in a council of priests: "What other man shall we find in whom the spirit of God is as in thee who can accomplish these things?" He therefore "consecrated him and bade him return in the Grace of God whence he came".

Frumentius accordingly returned to Axum as Ethiopia's first Christian bishop and there he continued his missionary endeavours – which were rewarded, eventually, by the conversion of the King himself. Afterwards, the new faith spread rapidly and the next two hundred years – during which Christianity established itself firmly as the State religion of Ethiopia – are regarded as a golden age. Towards the end of the sixth century AD, however, the port of Adulis was sacked. Barely one hundred years afterwards, Muslim invaders from Arabia seized and occupied much of the coastal zone. Deprived of its access to the sea, Axum then slumped with terrible rapidity into cultural and military stagnation – the beginnings of the millennial sleep that Gibbon was to describe.

Above: Carved wooden cross depicting the crucifixion.

FACING PAGE: Priest with fly whisk and staff on the ridge above Lalibela's river Jordan.

ABOVE: A nun emerging from the labyrinth of tunnels which connect the rock-hewn churches of Lalibela.
FACING PAGE: A priest standing at the entrance to a chiselled passageway.

SUCCEEDING PAGES: *Beta Ghiorghis*, (the House of St George), with its cruciform design, is carved out of the surrounding rock and stands more than 40 feet high. According to legend, St George came by night to supervise the construction work. It is said that the hoofprints of his horse can be seen to this day in the courtyard.

LEFT: A priest descends the stairway of the so-called "Tomb of Adam" constructed over the "Tomb of Eve" within the Lalibela complex of churches.

ABOVE: Detail of a keel-arched window in the church of Golgotha, Lalibela.

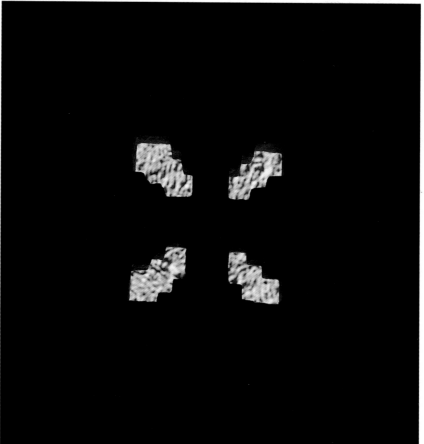

LEFT: A priest reads from the *Kidan* (New Testament) in the church of St Gabriel.

RIGHT: The rock-hewn churches of Lalibela are renowned for their window designs. The lower window, in the form of a swastika is believed to symbolize the Greek cross with bent arms, or, according to legend, the axe-shaped chisel which King Lalibela used to carve the churches. The centre and upper windows show some of the variety of the more familiar cross shapes.

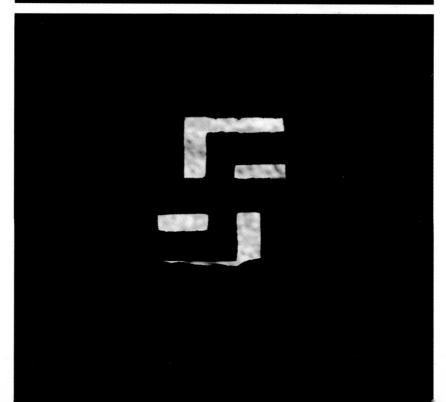

ABOVE: The Ethiopian Orthodox Church is still the centre of worship and community life in Ethiopia. In the courtyard of Beta Mariam a nun sifts wheat, the grain used for communion bread.

RIGHT: A pilgrim reads from the Psalms of David, the most popular prayer book in Ethiopia. His wooden cross is a reminder of the cross on which Jesus was crucified, and his staff symbolizes the rod with which Moses struck the rock in the wilderness to provide water for the children of Israel.

OVERLEAF (LEFT): A deacon reads from one of the old bibles still to be found in every church. These large wood and leather-bound volumes are hand written in *Ge'ez*, the ancient Semitic language of northern Ethiopia. Many are beautifully illuminated and some are centuries old. (RIGHT): Nuns rest in the courtyard of Geneta Mariam, a church situated in the mountains on the outskirts of Lalibela.

LEFT: The ninth-century church of Mekina Medahane Alem was built by King Alse Gabre Maskal three hundred years before the time of Lalibela. This church is not rock-hewn but was erected inside a cave high in the mountains.

ABOVE: Worn in procession by a young deacon, this gold-washed filigree crown symbolizes the crown of enlightenment.

LEFT: *Genna* (Christmas) occurs on 7 January according to Ethiopia's archaic Julian calendar and is one of the important celebrations of the Orthodox Church. Young deacons wear filigree crowns and embroidered capes which, when spread out, form the shape of a cross.

RIGHT: Each church has its own processional crosses, usually cast in bronze or brass. Crosses of these designs have been manufactured in Lalibela since at least the thirteenth century.

SUCCEEDING PAGES

(38 AND 39): *Timkat* (Epiphany) is the most important celebration of the Ethiopian Orthodox Church. It occurs twelve days after Christmas and celebrates the baptism of Christ by St John in the river Jordan. It is at this time that the holy *tabots* – representations of the original tablets of stone contained in the Ark of the Covenant, are taken from their respective churches and carried in procession to Lalibela's own river Jordan. The *tabots* are wrapped in silk brocade and carried on the heads of the priests, sheltered by velvet umbrellas representing the celestial spheres.

(40 AND 41): In the early hours of Christmas morning, priests bearing prayer shawls and carrying censors filled with frankincense and myrrh circle Lalibela's Beta Mariam church.

(42 AND 43): Under an awning in the sunken courtyard of Beta Mariam, priests gather to recite *Kinnae* (mystical poetry) in *Ge'ez*. It is chanted slowly to the accompaniment of drums and sistra (jingling metal rattles).

(44 AND 45): Priests surround the edge of the wall of Beta Mariam and, in antiphonal fashion, chant to the members of the congregation below – who then call their responses back. This ceremony symbolizes the harmony between heaven and earth, the dialogue between God and man.

(46 AND 47): These four senior priests are representatives of a line that stretches back to the fourth century when the Patriarch of Alexandria consecrated the Church in Ethiopia. The priests are elderly men and, due to the increasing impoverishment of the Church, fear that their ancient traditions may die with them.

CHAPTER TWO

THE HEAVENLY WORLD

Gondar: the Falasha and Amhara

outhward from Axum as far as the city of Gondar and Lake Tana a swarming army of giant mountains marches in almost unbroken ranks for tens of thousands of square miles. The ancient Greeks referred to this remote hill country as a "cool celestial island". Today its agricultural valleys and lofty plateaux are largely inhabited by peasant farmers.

The dominant group are the Amharas, a Semitic race whose forefathers are thought to have migrated to the Horn from Arabia thousands of years ago. An even older layer of peoples is also to be found here, however – indigenous Hamites known as the Agaw. Most are Christians, but some practise an archaic form of the Jewish faith and are called Falashas. Notable for their unique religious beliefs and their claims to past greatness, the Falashas are also the victims of widespread popular prejudice and of extreme poverty – all factors that, in the closing years of the twentieth century, have brought them to the very edge of extinction.

ETHIOPIAN JEWS

In their poor and simple villages in the Ethiopian highlands today, the Falashas might easily be mistaken for any other Abyssinian people. Indeed, even these villages themselves are not always separate: Falashas frequently live as the neighbours of the Amhara Christian – when they do so, however, their homes are normally arranged in a compact unit somewhat apart from the remainder of the settlement, a village within a village.

As regards physical appearance, there is little or nothing to distinguish Ethiopian Jews from Ethiopian gentiles. Socioeconomic differences, however, are considerable. Falasha men frequently work as blacksmiths, weavers and tanners, while the women make pots and baskets. By contrast, such lowly trades are avoided and despised by Christian Ethiopian highlanders – indeed, amongst the Amhara, the word for "manual worker" (*tabib*) has the same meaning as "one with the evil eye".[1]

The most important difference of all between the Falashas and their neighbours is, of course, religious. This difference marks these people out as a group apart, and contains the secret of their cultural survival.

The central feature of Falasha

LEFT: A painting of St Estateos (14th C), from the church of Debre Sina at Gorgora, Lake Tana.

religion, common to Jews everywhere, is a belief "in the one and only God, the God of Israel, who has chosen His people and who will send the Messiah to redeem them and return them to the Holy Land".[2] Like other Jews, too, the Falashas practice male circumcision on the morning of the eighth day after birth, are rigorous in their observance of the Sabbath, and pay meticulous attention to the laws of cleanliness and purity.

As regards food habits, the Falashas eat only the flesh of animals which both chew the cud and are cloven-hooved; they also obey the commandments governing birds and fish which are laid down in the Book of Leviticus. An animal slaughtered by a gentile will not under any circumstances be eaten by any Ethiopian Jew.

Turning to general religious observances, the most distinctive characteristic of the Falashas is that they adhere strictly to the teachings of the Torah (particularly the Pentateuch – the five books of Moses). This Written Law is regarded by them as nothing less than the revealed will of God. However, as might be expected of a Jewish people who appear to have been isolated from their co-religionists for almost two thousand years, they are completely unfamiliar with the Oral Law, the Halachah (known as the Talmud) – the codification of which was not completed until around 500 AD.

It is equally a consequence of this isolation that the Torah used by the Falashas is written not in Hebrew but in *Ge'ez* (which is also the liturgical language of the Ethiopian Orthodox Church). Indeed, it seems probable that the Falasha have *never* spoken Hebrew – though they are familiar with a few Hebrew words occurring mainly in prayers.

Falasha synagogues are called *masgid* (a word that means "mosque" amongst Islamic peoples), and are typically small, undistinguished round or square buildings with two entrances – of which one is set into the eastern wall, the supposed direction of the city of Jerusalem. The Torah (inscribed on parchment made of the skin of edible animals) is also usually found on this eastern wall, where it is placed on a board decorated with multicoloured drapes. As in the days of the first Temple, Ethiopia's Jews do not have rabbis (who are essentially teachers), but rather priests (*Cahenat*) whose responsibility it is to conduct religious ceremonies and who claim descent from Aaron.[3]

The Falashas celebrate the new moons and the majority of Jewish festivals as prescribed in the Pentateuch. Passover, for example, is commemorated from the fifteenth to the twenty-first days of the first moon of the year and a sacrifical lamb is offered on the eve of this festival.

Curiously, Ethiopia's Jews regard the weekly Sabbath not simply as a day of rest but also, and more importantly, as a *holy person*. This metaphysical being is female and is seen as the manifestation on earth of the heavenly world – to which end she is given names: "Luminous", "Vivifying", "Rejoicing" and "Beloved". She constantly intercedes with God on behalf of both the righteous and the sinners, reminding the Almighty that she is a "sign" and a witness to the people.[4]

Preparations for the Sabbath begin on Friday afternoons: women wash their bodies and their clothing, prepare beer, grind grain and bake bread; men cease their work at midday and also wash. All fires are extinguished after sunset and darkness falls amid an almost eerie silence. On the Sabbath itself no work of any kind is done, no water may be drawn, no fire lit and no coffee boiled. Although there is no fasting (except when the Sabbath and the Day of Atonement coincide), only cold food and drink are permissible. Quarrelling is strictly forbidden and the usual form of greeting is *sanbat salaam, sanbat salaam* (Sabbath peace, Sabbath peace). It appears that in ancient times the Falashas even observed the restrictions of the Sabbath when they were at war – only fighting to defend themselves if they were attacked.

A HISTORY OF PERSECUTION

The Falashas have been forced to go to war often during their long history. At first they were on the offensive. Indeed, in the tenth century, the larger Agaw group to which they belong was responsible for the final downfall of the Axumite empire. Under a formidable chieftainess called Gudit (or Judith) these Hamitic peoples attacked Axum, razed much of the ancient city, overthrew its last king, killed the royal princes – thus interrupting the Solomonic line – and tried to uproot the Christian faith.

In Ethiopia today, Gudit is most often remembered as a monster – a heathen whose hatred of Christianity was so profound that she destroyed every church that her armies came across. She can also be seen, however, as a champion of the Hamitic inhabitants of the highlands: her campaign brought to an end a very long period of domination by the Semitic rulers of Axum. Subsequently secular power shifted southward from Tigray into Wollo, a move that is seen by scholars as "a necessary step in the integration of Abyssinia . . . the Agaw people, hitherto subject to a Semitic or Semitized aristocracy, now gained the upper hand, and the distinctions of descent or class between rulers and ruled began to disappear."[5]

Left: Falasha clay figurine depicting King Solomon and the Queen of Sheba (encased in an egg) conceiving Menelik I, the first emperor of Ethiopia.
Above: Solomon and Sheba in the act of conception.
Below: The Lion of Judah.

There is, furthermore, evidence to suggest that Gudit was *not* a pagan upstart but rather a monotheistic conservative motivated by a desire to restore the Jewish faith to its former prominence in her country. Historians now accept that Judaism established itself in Ethiopia long before the coming of Christianity.[6] Quite how it arrived is by no means clear – although the Falashas claim they are the descendants of the bodyguard provided by King Solomon to accompany Menelik on his journey from Jerusalem.[7]

If Gudit's objective was indeed to bring about a resurgence of Judaism, however, then she failed. By the mid-twelfth century the majority of the Agaw had converted to Christianity and King Lalibela was at work building his remarkable rock-hewn churches. Slightly more than a hundred years after that – in 1270 – the Solomonic dynasty was restored.

Thereafter, Ethiopia's Jews were subjected to increasingly violent attacks by their Christian monarchs. This period of persecution, which lasted for almost half a millennium, only makes sense if we accept that Judaism was seen as a real threat to the legitimacy and power of the Solomonic Emperors.

This also perhaps explains why so many anti-Jewish sentiments flavour the liturgy of the Ethiopian Orthodox Church and also the wording of the *Kebra Nagast*, the national saga compiled from oral sources in the fourteenth century: in the former we are told that the Jews are the "assassins of Christ", in the latter that they are the "enemies of God". The various royal chronicles which record the achievements of successive Emperors contain similar accusations: during Amda Sion's rule for example (1314–44) Jews were referred to as "renegades", "crucifiers" and "former Christians who denied Christ".

Sarsa Dengel, the Solomonic Emperor who ruled from 1563 to 1594, waged a seventeen-year campaign against the Jews. During the fighting, which saw brutal onslaughts against Falasha strongholds in the Simien mountains, the defenders acquitted themselves with great dignity. Even Sarsa Dengel's sycophantic chronicler could not avoid expressing admiration for the courage of one group of Jewish women who, rather than be captured and used by the Emperor's troops, hurled themselves off a cliff with the cry "Adonai, help me".[8]

The next period of severe persecution of the Falasha people began in 1607 when Emperor Susneyos ascended the throne. On the advice of a group of Portuguese Jesuits who had installed themselves at his court, he launched a pogrom against all Jews living in the highlands between Lake Tana and the Simien mountains. During the next twenty years, thousands were killed in fierce fighting and their children were sold as slaves.

Neither Susneyos nor his Jesuit advisers were to enjoy their triumph for very long, however. When the Emperor abandoned the Orthodox Church and adopted Catholicism there were widespread revolts amongst his Christian subjects. In 1632, as a result, he was forced to abdicate in favour of his son Fasilidas – whose first act as monarch was to expel the Jesuit missionaries from Ethiopia.

St Gabre Manfras Kiddus, riding on a red bird representing thunder, holds in his arms a small man – his most loyal friend.

The departure of the Jesuits and the restoration of the Orthodox Church, undoubtedly saved Ethiopia from the negative effects of further foreign intervention. The new Emperor, furthermore, proved to be an imaginative and fair-minded man who is remembered as one of his country's greatest leaders. The return to social justice that he pioneered, however, could not undo the damage already inflicted on Abyssinia's Jews. As a result, in the centuries that followed, their numbers steadily declined – from perhaps half a million in the early 1600s to less than thirty thousand in 1984.[9] This process was greatly accelerated in the famine year of 1985 when some seven thousand Falashas were airlifted to Israel in the widely publicized "Operation Moses".[10]

As a result of this latter-day exodus, and of earlier and subsequent emigrations, there are now thought to be some fifteen thousand Falashas living in Israel – more, ironically and sadly, than linger in Ethiopia itself. Despite all the odds, however, despite a long history of persecution, despite the social pressures to "disappear" that inevitably bear down powerfully on a dwindling and distinctively "different" minority, despite the pernicious efforts of Christian missionaries,[11] despite famine, and despite deepening, demoralizing poverty, a single, undeniable and uplifting truth remains: the Falasha people still hold on to a strong and individual "idea" of themselves and, in the Abyssinian highlands, they continue to this day to proclaim their confidence in the God of Israel and in His Commandments.

THE AMHARA ETHIC

The few Falasha communities still remaining in Ethiopia are to be found around the shores of Lake Tana, in the vicinity of the city of Gondar – and northwards from there towards the Simien mountains. This extensive Afro-Alpine zone is populated in the main by Amharas, a vigorous, competitive, and hard-working Christian people who, throughout history, have had a profound impact not only on the Falashas but also on many of the other ethnic groups with whom they have come into contact. Over a period of more than seven hundred years, from 1270 until 1974, all but one of the rulers of Ethiopia were Amharas. It was their mother tongue, furthermore – Amharic – that was adopted as Ethiopia's *lingua franca*: as a result, with the single exception of Arabic, it now has more speakers than any other Semitic language in the world.

Like their forefathers for countless generations, the Amharas are predominantly simple peasants whose lives are ruled by the iron rods of soil and season. Long ago detribalized, the prime attachments of each individual are to his land and home, to his own immediate kin and to God.

The seemingly boundless mountain panoramas are dotted with small hamlets – usually of six houses or less – that are generally inhabited by single extended families. The traditional dwelling is round with walls made of wattle and daub or sometimes of stone, and with a conical thatched roof that is supported by a wooden pole rising through the centre. This circular design is also taken up in the numerous churches that are everywhere to be seen; these, however, tend to be larger and more imposing than ordinary houses and are further distinguished by the presence of two concentric partitions inside, the innermost of which – the Holy of Holies – is restricted to priests and deacons and contains the sacred *tabots* (the Tablets of the Law).

In this intensely conservative rural culture, farm labour is idealized and is thought to enshrine the timeless virtues of independence and honesty. There is, in addition, a stubborn resistance to modernizing influences, partly because the peasant's poverty prevents him from exploring alternative ways of doing things, partly because he does not want to undertake such explorations. The notion of *eddil* (fate) linked to the ineffable will of God is particularly strong and discourages families from making determined efforts to influence their environment. "If a man works hard," as one typical farmer expressed it, "he may remain poor. If he does not work hard, he may become wealthy. The outcome is due to fate."[12]

Such attitudes do not promote laziness but rather an unquestioning acceptance of the backbreaking drudgery involved in traditional means of winning a living from a harsh and uncompromising land. The toil, however, is not entirely unremitting: Saturdays and Sundays are both honoured as the Sabbath by the majority of rural Amharas. On these days – and on many others which are dedicated to the commemoration of important Saints – men may not plough or harvest, women may not grind or spin. Weddings and christenings are always taken as occasions for huge feasts and merrymaking. The year is also punctuated by several very large-scale festivals.

The first of these, New Year, falls on 11 September according to Ethiopia's archaic Julian calendar.[13] This occasion, known as *Engutatash*, also marks St John's Day and comes near the end of the long rainy season: in good times, when there is no drought, peasant homes are luxuriantly strewn with green freshly cut grass, and groups of singing children are to be seen moving from house to house with bunches of wild flowers.

The next festival, *Maskal*, is celebrated sixteen days later on 27 September. It marks the finding by Empress Helena (the mother of Constantine the Great) of the true Cross on which Jesus was crucified. As a historical event, the discovery of the cross in fact occurred on 19 March 326. Ethiopians, however, celebrate it much later in the year – almost certainly because, in very ancient times, the end of September with its bright fresh weather was the occasion for the pagan spring rites. A syncretization of heathen and Christian traditions, *Maskal* thus occurs at a moment when the rural landscape is overgrown with the bright yellow daisies that appear everywhere in the highlands after the rains. Families cut these flowers and attach them to poles which are then brought to a central clearing where they form the tepeelike framework for a huge bonfire. In the afternoon priests intone chants and members of the community circle around the bonfire – which, however, is not lit until the evening. As on almost all other festive occasions there is much consumption of *tella*, the local millet beer.

Christmas comes in early January. Its Amharic name, *Genna*, is also applied to a rather rough and aggressive game that is played with sticks and a wooden puck on the same day. Christmas is not, as in Europe, the paramount religious festival of the year; indeed it is in many respects a secular event. The utmost importance, however, is conferred upon *Timkat* (Epiphany), which commemorates the baptism of Christ and which is celebrated in its most elaborate form amongst the rock-hewn churches of Lalibela.[14] *Timkat* marks the beginning of a season of weddings and feasting during February and March – a season that is brought to an abrupt end by the eight-week-long fast that precedes Easter. In mid-May, during the final week of Lent, no heavy work is allowed and church-going becomes the principal daily activity; complete abstinence from both food and sex is called for in the forty-eight hours before the final Mass which takes place in the middle of the night prior to *Fasika* – Easter day itself.

There are numerous other fasts and festivals throughout the year of the Amhara peasant; some of these events are major, some are minor – but most families try to participate to the maximum extent possible in all of these recurring communal celebrations. Even in the midst of great hardship and hunger they will continue to starve themselves if that is what the season requires; even though virtually crippled by poverty they will do their utmost to provide generous feasts at the appropriate times.

Festivals and holidays see the Amhara at their most convivial and sociable. Such occasions, however, are the exception rather than the rule – for these are folk who accord a particularly high value to the concept of rugged individualism. Reflected in the peasant's dislike of gregarious village life, this ideal finds its ultimate expression in a willingness to undertake the long and sometimes hazardous journeys that the terrain demands. The image of the iron-sinewed farmer setting out for distant places with his loins girded up and his hardwood *dula* (staff) braced across his shoulders is thus one that holds a special romantic appeal for all Amharas.

There is, however, another important aspect to the character of these people that

Disciples of St Yared (founder of Ethiopian church music) singing for King Gabre Maskal in Axum.

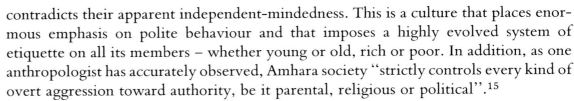

contradicts their apparent independent-mindedness. This is a culture that places enormous emphasis on polite behaviour and that imposes a highly evolved system of etiquette on all its members – whether young or old, rich or poor. In addition, as one anthropologist has accurately observed, Amhara society "strictly controls every kind of overt aggression toward authority, be it parental, religious or political".[15]

It is in this context that the absolute power exercised by the many Amharic Emperors who have ruled Ethiopia is best understood. Furthermore, it is precisely to this orderly and essentially unchallengeable despotism that the Amhara owe their enormous success in the turbulent arena of the Horn of Africa. Where other peoples have been anarchic, riven by tribal conflicts and thus quite unable to realize their own potential, the Amhara have constantly drawn upon their own collective strength to extend their sphere of influence. The fruits of this have not only been great political and economic power for the few whose fortune it has been to rise to the top of an extremely hierarchical social structure, but also the emergence of a material and artistic culture of considerable scope and grandeur.

GONDAR THE BEAUTIFUL

This culture is best expressed in the graceful city of Gondar, founded by the Emperor Fasilidas in the year 1635. Standing at the considerable altitude of 7,000 feet, flanked by twin mountain streams, Gondar commands spectacular views over descending layers of agricultural countryside as far as Lake Tana some 40 miles to the south. At the centre of the city is an extensive walled compound which contains the hulking ruins of a group of imposing castles – the most significant of which was built in the middle of the seventeenth century on the orders of Fasilidas himself. This Emperor, who was greatly interested in architecture, was also responsible for seven churches, a number of bridges, and a three-storey stone pavilion positioned next to a large sunken bathing place, which, even today, is still filled up with water from a nearby river during the *Timkat* season.

Iyasu the Great, a grandson of Fasilidas, was another great builder. His most lasting achievement was the church of Debre Berhan Selassie, Mount of the Light of the Trinity, which stands surrounded by a high wall on raised ground to the northwest of the city – and which continues to be in regular use. A plain, thatched, rectangular structure on the outside, the interior of Debre Berhan Selassie is marvellously painted with a great variety of scenes from religious history. The spaces between the beams of the ceiling contain the brilliant wide-eyed images of more than eighty angels' faces – all of which are different, individual, with their own character and expressions. The north wall, into which is set the Holy of Holies, is dominated by a powerful depiction of the Trinity above a crucified Christ. The theme of the south wall is St Mary and that of the east wall the life of Jesus. The west wall shows important saints, with St George in red and gold mounted on a prancing white horse.

IMAGES OF HEAVEN

While Gondar remained the capital of Ethiopia – and it did so until 1855 – it was a vital centre of religious learning and of all the arts. Here, despite the political and economic decline that set in during the eighteenth century, painting and music, dance and poetry – together with the facilities and expertise for skilled instruction in all these and many other disciplines – continued to thrive for more than two hundred years.

Historians recognize two principal stylistic epochs in Ethiopian art. The first of these is known as the "medieval" and encapsulates an approach to painting that had its origins in the very remote past; the main surviving exemplars date roughly from the thirteenth to the early sixteenth centuries. The second period, which is referred to as "Gondarene", began in the seventeenth century with the founding of the city; this period, despite the subsequent introduction of a number of important innovations, extends right up to modern times.

Prince Gabre Kristos, having left home to pursue the religious way of life, returns to the palace disguised as a beggar and is recognized only by his dogs.

At some risk of oversimplification it is fair to say that Ethiopian painting of the medieval school was dominated by Byzantine influences. By contrast, the identifying hallmark of the Gondarene period is an increasingly realistic and "Western European" approach. The layman confronted with a collection of Ethiopian paintings dating from several widely separated centuries, however, is more likely to be struck by the essential similarities that link the works than by any superficial stylistic changes.

Religious themes dominate all but the most recent of Ethiopian art. This is hardly surprising since painting was introduced into the country along with Christianity. In the early years the Holy Scriptures were imported exclusively from the Byzantine world and, naturally, were illuminated in the Byzantine style; thereafter, from generation to generation, they were translated and recopied in Ethiopian churches and monasteries.

Even after the foundation of Gondar, scriptural themes maintained their importance in Ethiopian art; the range of stories told, however, increased dramatically. The Virgin Mary became a popular subject as did the lives and acts of the Saints. Stylistically, there was a willingness to adopt new models – for example Renaissance or Baroque paintings – emanating from the expansive and powerful Western civilizations with which Ethiopia increasingly came into contact from the sixteenth century onwards as the Portuguese and other visitors began to arrive.

"Naturalism" became more acceptable and a conscious effort was made by at least some artists to depart from stiff and geometrical Byzantine lines: perspective and relief were introduced, together with motion and elaborate details. The new realism also brought with it an eagerness to depict the Ethiopian way of life: thus surrounding even the most "spiritual" subjects one may sometimes distinguish the presence of everyday objects such as houses, weapons and baskets. Most notable of all is the manner in which the personalities depicted in the best Gondarene works are not flat and inanimate as before but rather are full of life: eyes that would previously have been immobile start to move in different directions, bodies to bend, hands to express feeling.

It is precisely these lifelike qualities – combined with a Baroque richness of design, a warmth of colour and a careful finish – that distinguish the dazzling paintings of the Debre Berhan Selassie church in Gondar and the paintings on the walls of the church of Debre Sina in Gorgora, an ancient settlement on the northern shores of Lake Tana.

Further paintings of equally fine quality adorn the twenty or so monasteries sheltered on Lake Tana's thirty-seven islands. Surviving remnants of a very old contemplative tradition, these remote religious communities have frequently been used during times of trouble as places of safety for art treasures and for religious relics from all parts of the country.

With a surface area of 1,418 square miles, Tana is Ethiopia's largest lake. Known to the ancient Greeks as Pseboa or Koloe,[16] its sometimes stormy waters are traversed by papyrus reed boats which differ little from those depicted on the tombs of the Pharaohs. Appropriately enough – on its way to enrich Egypt's fertile delta – it is out of this same lake that the Blue Nile river flows with tremendous force and volume over the basalt shoulder of a giant cataract and onwards from there, ever downwards through dark and angry defiles, towards the deserts of the Sudan.

For millions of Ethiopian Christians, the Blue Nile, even today, is thought of as the Ghion of Genesis 2.13 – "the second river" that "compasseth the whole land of Abyssinia".[17] Surrounded by high mountains, a shrine for churches and monasteries, a home for the devout and a repository for transcendent works of art, Lake Tana is thus nothing less than the sublime eye of a heavenly world and the heart of the ancient civilization of the highlands.

One of the first saints to bring Christianity to Ethiopia was given a snake by God to help him climb the formidable escarpment on top of which he built the church of Debre Damo.

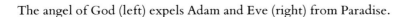

The angel of God (left) expels Adam and Eve (right) from Paradise.

LEFT: A priest, with processional cross and illuminated manuscript, stands at the entrance to the Holy of Holies in the sixteenth-century church of Ura Kidane Mehret on Lake Tana.

ABOVE: The church of Debre Berhan Selassie in Gondar was built during the reign of King Fasilidas in the seventeenth century. The canvases are affixed directly on to the walls and ceiling. They depict the Holy Trinity, equestrian saints and religious heroes.

OVERLEAF: The ceiling of Debre Berhan Selassie is covered with paintings of archangels whose eyes are believed to follow the faithful as they come to prayer. A strong Byzantine influence is plainly visible.

ABOVE: Equestrian saints, Estateos and Fasilidas, chasing unbelievers out of Gondar. BELOW: Filatios destroying subjects of Pagan worship. Both paintings (17th C.) are from the church of Ura Kidane Mehret, Lake Tana.

ABOVE: Abadir and Abole chasing Catholics or Muslims from the Christian capitol, from the Church of Ura Kidane Mehret.
BELOW: George, patron saint of Ethiopia, slaying the dragon (19th C.), from the church of Debre Berhan Selassie in Gondar.

61

ሰቋዘ፡ ኀቡዩ፡ ብሰሰ፡ የሞወበሊ፡ ዒቀ፡ ሰ፡ልፎ፡መ፡ ኀቡ፡ የቡሰ፡ ዖለ፡ደ

PRECEDING PAGES: In this twentieth-century Gondar painting twenty-four elders wearing filigree crowns and swinging incense burners approach the throne of God.

LEFT: St Gabre Manfas Kiddus crossed the desert preaching peace to wild beasts of prey. When he found a bird dying of thirst he allowed it to drink water from his eye. Legend has it that he wandered for three hundred years before being called to sit next to God in heaven. This twentieth-century painting, which stands in Addis Ababa's Cathedral of St George, is by the well-known contemporary artist Afewerk Tekle.

ABOVE: "The Animals Banquet" is a twentieth-century painting by the artist Hailu. It symbolizes the union of the animals in friendship and love. In the beginning, the animals preyed upon one another, but when God revealed to them that their plight was the work of the devil, they united to kill their oppressor. Institute of Ethiopian Studies, Addis Ababa.

OVERLEAF: Gondar, capital city of Ethiopia in the seventeenth century, with the castle and walled compound built by King Fasilidas.

PRECEDING PAGES: Peasant farmers and artisans, the Falasha
– who call themselves *Beta Israel* (House of Israel) are indigenous Ethiopian Jews. Their origins are cloaked in mystery.

LEFT: Falasha women are skilled in pottery. They make clay
figurines depicting various legends from the history of
Judaism. The Star of David is a pan-Judaic symbol believed
to bring good luck.

ABOVE: Figurine of a *Cahen* (Priest) carrying the Torah.

ABOVE: Inside their synagogue, elders in a Falasha village celebrate *Rosh Hashanah*, the Jewish New Year, by sharing a special feast of *injera* (sour pancakes) with *wat* (spicy meat sauce).

LEFT: A Falasha *Cahen*, holding the Old Testament.

LEFT: A Falasha *Telleq Cahen* (High Priest) carrying the Torah wrapped in red and white cloth.

ABOVE: The Torah is a handwritten parchment scroll containing the five books of Moses. It is read throughout the year, starting with Genesis and ending with the arrival of the Hebrews in the promised land. Its cloth cover is decorated with the Ten Commandments written in Hebrew.

CHAPTER THREE

THE DESERT AT THE MOUNTAINS' FEET

Peoples of Eritrea and the Rift Valley

uring the primordial eruptions that forged Ethiopia's highlands, so much volcanic material was spewed forth that the earth's crust was critically weakened along two roughly parallel faults. These were not confined to the Horn but extended nearly 3,750 miles from what is now Syria in the north, to Mozambique in the far south. Some twenty million years ago, along the full length of the corridor between the fault lines, the land collapsed; as it did so it formed the deep depression that is now known as the Great Rift Valley.

The Eritrean coast and the sun-blackened lava deserts of the Djibouti Republic trace the wide contours of this colossal geological trench where it first enters the African mainland. Overlooked from the west by the soaring cliff wall of the Abyssinian escarpment, the volcanic floor of the Rift is one of our planet's most hostile environments. There are many points where midday temperatures, even in the shade, exceed 135 degrees Fahrenheit. Yellow sulphur fields pit the terrain and earthquakes are frequently felt. Boiling springs well up here and there giving off clouds of steam, and there are several active volcanoes – dying reminders of the furies that once raged here.

This unfriendly corner of the Horn of Africa appears to be inimical to the human species. By contrast with the cool green tablelands of the Abyssinian massif, there is almost nothing here able to support life; in every direction, as far as the eye can see, desolation extends; the air is almost too hot to breathe; sometimes there are no sounds – not a voice, not a bird's song, not the hum of an insect's wings – just a vast, empty, silence.

People do live here, however – Hamitic tribesmen whose nomadic existence marks them out as the hardiest of Noah's sturdy sons. These vagabond herders are a warrior race. Though they call themselves Afar, they are perhaps better known as the Danakil – an epithet that is also applied to their daunting homelands, which are frequently referred to as Dankalia.

The smallest and most typical Afar camps are called *burra* and are made up of just one or two portable dome-shaped huts consisting of skins stretched over curved armatures of stick and housing parts of a patrilineal extended family. On the rare occasions when the rangelands are green, relatively big encampments of up to one hundred people may be seen.

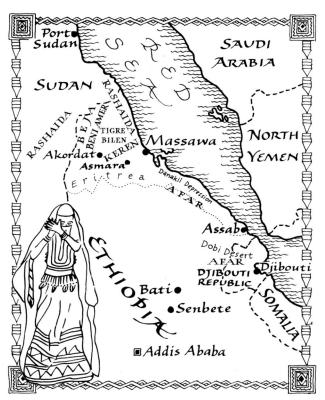

LEFT: An Afar nomad stands amid razor-edged limestone stalagmites overlooking Lake Abbe in Djibouti.

Notions of community in such a setting are inevitably very different from those held by city dwellers, or even by rural villagers. Lacking fixed property, or the various codified rules and regulations of a settled civilization, fierce loyalties to clan and to tribe assume great significance; indeed such loyalties are often the only adhesives binding the Afars together.

Tribal territories are demarcated by boundaries which follow natural features such as dried-out river beds, hills and rocks. Clans, as tribal sub-units, are then subdivided in turn into a number of lineages.

Every clan has its own chief, whose duties include rainmaking, and also a spokesman. These patriarchs, together with their counterparts from other clans, form the convocation of elders which is the most important legislative body in a culture bound by the Mosaic edict of an "eye for an eye and a tooth for a tooth".

LOVE OF LIVESTOCK

A people superbly adapted to their environment, the Afar derive their livelihood from animal husbandry. Sheep, goats and cattle are all herded. It is the ownership of camels, however, that is accorded the greatest esteem.

Although camels may be slaughtered and eaten on special occasions, and although their milk is highly prized, they are never ridden; their principal role, rather, is as pack animals. Rapid mobility is more than just a dimension of the nomads' cherished freedom; in the unmerciful terrain of the Rift it is life itself. Afar families rely totally on their camels to carry their possessions, including the heavy constituent parts of their huts – the most distinctive features of which are the curved wooden frames which are bound in clusters within rolled-up mats when the nomads are on the move.

The patrilineal extended family is the unit responsible for almost all aspects of animal husbandry in Afar society. Herding chores are shared out amongst various family members. Each married woman, for example, has her own mixed flock of goats and sheep (sometimes divided into two separate flocks), which she tends with the help of her young children. Cattle and camels, on the other hand, are the property of the men who constantly seek to increase the size of their herds, and thus their own wealth: a single camel has an exchange value of fifty or sixty goats.

So important are livestock that every new-born child – boy or girl – is given a present of one female animal of each species. This gift, known as *hundubta* (navel-string), becomes the basis of the full-scale herd that each individual will subsequently endeavour to build up. The majority of Afar will never own any other productive asset; their livestock supply them with their staple foods in the form of milk and meat, and also their luxuries – like butter mixed in yoghurt.

Livestock and livestock products like milk, hides and skins have an additional and equally vital role to play. These items may be sold to raise money, or else bartered directly for needed items like grain and vegetables, neither of which are grown by the nomads. Virtually the only other tradeable commodity of Dankalia is natural salt which some Afar tribes mine in the below-sea-level crucible of the Dallol Depression and in the Dobi Desert.

There are two principal markets – Senbete and Bati – both of which are situated in the foothills of the escarpment at an altitude of some 5,200 feet above the Rift's baking floor. Here the trade of the mountains comes down to meet the trade of the plains: on the one hand chickens, eggs, grains, vegetables, spices, clothing and shoes – together with luxury items like soap, aluminium cooking utensils, cigarettes, tobacco, and jewelry; on the other cattle, camels, goats, sheep, part-cured hides, bars of rock salt, and containers of milk and *ghee* (clarified butter). The scene is a kaleidoscope of contrasts – the mixed fragrances of incense, drying skins, cow dung and camels; the sounds of people haggling in a variety of languages; and the striking differences of appearance between the highlanders and the nomads.

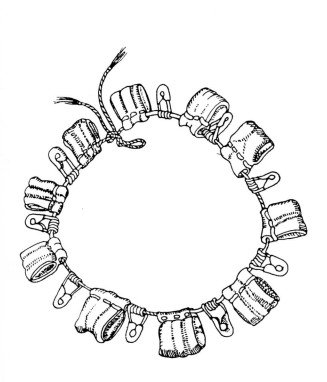

BEAUTIFUL KILLERS

Afar women, in their youth, are dark-eyed and mysterious: long, graceful necks, sensuous mouths and delicate features are combined with a stately and elegant bearing. In their teenaged, marriageable years they seem to rise, however briefly, above the rigours of desert life to achieve a transcendental loveliness.

Hair is carefully combed and arranged in a series of hanging ringlets. Clothing, however, is austere. Virgins go bare-breasted, but wrap their hips and legs in long cloth skirts dyed brown with an extract of mimosa bark. After marriage a black shawl of transparent cotton voile (the *shash*, or *mushal*) is worn around the head, and sometimes draped over the shoulders. The main and most popular female adornments are simple in the extreme: coloured beads and leather thongs, together with metal rings, bangles and anklets. Tatooing and body scarification are also popular decorations, and most of the women bear tribal marks on their faces.

Afar men are renowned for their vanity; their hair, frizzled rather than tightly curled, is normally teased out into a fuzzy mop – or else liberally annointed with *ghee* and woven into close shiny ringlets. As with the women, body and facial scarifications are frequently encountered; in addition the upper front teeth are filed down.

Tough hide sandals are the most common footwear; the other male garments are an ankle-length cotton sarong belted at the waist and a light toga drawn around the upper body. A hardwood staff is always carried. Strapped left to right in a leather sheath that lies across the front of the stomach, the wickedly sharp curved knife known as the *jile* is worn by all Afar men.

"The Danakil," as one European traveller put it, "kill any stranger at sight; the taking of life has become a habit of their nature."[1] From earliest childhood – when their only toys are small bows and arrows – Afar males are imbued with an ethic of extreme violence. Even at play, aggression is considered a paramount virtue: in *kwosso*, a ball game traditionally played by teams of warriors one hundred strong, serious injuries and even deaths may occur.

In a world in which might is right and in which true prestige is accorded only to those who are manifestly strong and successful, it is little wonder that men grow up convinced it "is better to die than to live without killing".[2] Indeed, intertribal homicide occupies such an important place in Afar society that males of all ages adorn themselves with external symbols of their prowess: a comb or a feather in the hair denote one kill; two kills entitle a warrior to split his ears; ten kills confer the right to wear a coveted iron bracelet. Other badges of glory include brass-bound leather thongs attached to knife or rifle – one for each successful murder.

ISLAM LIGHTLY WORN

Although the Afar profess themselves to be Muslims, it is true to say that Islam sits but lightly upon them. As one scholar has rightly observed, they are a people who "do not hold God in any great awe . . . They think of Him not as an omnipotent King, His powers are so obviously limited, but rather as a great *shaikh* worthy of following if He shows qualities of leadership and generosity."[3]

It is probable that Islam was introduced to Dankalia in the tenth century by wandering holy men from Arabia. The success of the new faith in the early years would have depended crucially on its ability to adapt itself to the far older established religion of the Sky-God *Waq*. This religion was at one time widespread amongst all the Hamitic peoples of the Horn and is still practised by some groups in Ethiopia – notably the Oromo (see Chapter Six).[4]

Amongst the Afar, close relatives of the Oromo, the conversion to Islam was probably achieved by a deliberate effort on the part of the missionaries to identify Waq, the

Leather talisman necklaces worn for protection by Afar men.

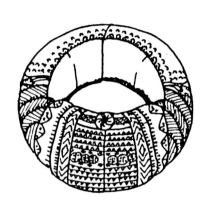

Silver jewellery. From top to bottom: bracelets worn by Rashaida women, anklet traded from Zanzibar, anklets worn by Beja and Rashaida women, and anklets worn by Rashaida women.

Father of the Universe, with Allah the one and only God. Rather than the latter abruptly replacing the former, it is thought that the two deities gradually merged in Afar minds over a period of several centuries. In consequence the religion of Dankalia today is characterized by a rich and revealing syncretism: on the surface orthodox Islam; just underneath, the cult of the Sky-God.

PROUD SURVIVORS

It is by no means beyond the bounds of possibility that Afar groups very similar to those of the late twentieth century were to be found in Dankalia as long ago as one thousand and perhaps even two thousand years BC. This is certainly the case with another closely related Hamitic people – the Beja, whose homelands also lie in the Rift along the Red Sea littoral, extending northwards from the edge of Afar territory and straddling the border between Eritrea and the Sudan.

According to one of their own most learned elders, "The Beja are descended from Kush, son of Ham, son of Noah."[5] A confederation of nomadic tribes, their principal sections today are the Besharin, the Amrar, the Bilen, the Tigray, the Hadendowa and the Beni Amer. Some have intermingled with the Semitic peoples of the highlands and have abandoned their original languages in the process; the majority, however, still retain the pure Hamitic *To Badawie* tongue and preserve their ancient traditions in an unadulterated form.

Like the Afar, the Beja are a handsome race – their skin tones vary from copper-red to deep brown and they typically have narrow noses, thin lips and fine Caucasian features. In manner they are frequently standoffish. "They speak to no strangers," remarked Diodorus Siculus who travelled among them in the first century BC, "they are interested in nothing."[6] A much later visitor, Rudyard Kipling, thought them vain and described the tough and surly Beja men as "Fuzzy-Wuzzies" on account of their "hayrick heads of hair". This style – an exaggerated Afro painstakingly teased out into mud-caked ringlets – is still in vogue today. More surprisingly, there is evidence that it was equally popular four thousand years ago: a tomb chapel in upper Egypt dating from the XIIth Pharaohonic Dynasty (1900 BC) bears what one authority describes as a "striking representation of a Fuzzy tribesman . . . showing the slender limbs, pointed nose, retracted abdomen, broad chest and the great shock hair of the modern Beshari or Hadendowi."[7]

Proud survivors, the Beja are warlike in defence of their tribal lands. In the nineteenth century, Hadendowa and Amrar fighters armed with spears and fearsome Abyssinian broadswords proved to be formidable opponents of British expansion in the Sudan. During the Mahdist uprising it was Beja warriors, some barely in their teens, who crept nightly between the lines to knife the British sentries and who charged unflinchingly into a hail of death and devastation on half a dozen battlefields.

At the Battle of Omdurman, in 1898, Beja foot soldiers faced the last cavalry charge ever mounted by the British army. Though force of arms ensured that the tribesmen were conclusively defeated, they nevertheless acquitted themselves honourably against the mounted troops. In just two minutes five officers, 65 men and 119 horses out of 400 were killed or wounded.

At Omdurman, as in previous battles, the Beja were only lightly armed: few of them had guns; some were equipped only with their heavy camel sticks – which they used with devastating effect against the legs of the horses.

Such reckless bravery seems to be characteristic of all the Hamitic warrior peoples of the Horn of Africa; brimming over with wild anger, vigorous in their hatred of interlopers, they have ever been adamant in the preservation of their freedom, their virility and their independence.

The nature of the country in which the Beja live undoubtedly nourishes such haughty and self-reliant individualism: the sparse rangelands and infrequent rains of the

Red Sea Hills make large population groupings impossible; rather – as is the case with the Afar – separation and isolation are the norm. Once again it is the patrilineal extended family that is the most important unit of tribal life and once again we encounter a scattered, aloof, itinerant people.

Some authorities do not hesitate to ascribe a certain nobility of character to the Beja; others detect only idleness. In reality both traits are probably present in significant quantities. Certainly, when not at war, the preferred activity of the menfolk – while dignified – is undemanding in the extreme: "They sit in the exiguous shade of their prized acacias watching their attenuated herds at graze and priding themselves that they are overlords of countless leagues of country, exempted for ever from the degrading necessity of manual labour."[8]

This relaxed patrician behaviour is so inimical to the acquisition of wealth that even the nomads' most prized asset – their livestock – remains to this day a substantially underdeveloped, and uncommercialized, resource. Renowned throughout northeastern Africa for the excellence of the camels that they breed, the Beja nevertheless seem utterly uninterested in the commercial value of their livestock. Indeed they have allowed recent interlopers from Saudi Arabia – the gypsy tribe known as the Rashaida – to monopolize the lucrative camel trade with Egypt.

SOME PARCEL OF ARABIA. . .

Quite distinct from the Hamitic Beja, the Rashaida are a Semitic people – the descendants of Noah's other son. Their presence in the Ethio-Sudanese borderlands dates back only to 1846 when, after losing a dispute with other more powerful Saudi clans, they fled their original homelands in the Hedjaz and crossed the Red Sea.[9]

Still quarrelsome today, the Rashaida have fared well in the Horn of Africa. Although they are surrounded on all sides by hostile Beja – and are in more or less constant conflict with the Hadendowa in particular – they have managed to achieve a certain measure of prosperity thanks to their acute business sense and their willingness to work hard. Camped out all their lives on the stark desert trails between Eritrea, Sudan and the camel markets of Egypt, their existence seems to symbolize in pure form the Bedouin ideals of their Arab forebears. Furthermore they have kept in close contact with their relatives on the other side of the Red Sea – with whom they trade for the elaborate Saudi and Yemeni jewellery much favoured by their womenfolk.

Collecting such presents from an early age, Rashaida women are often so weighed down with ornaments by the time they marry that they can hardly move. Additional gifts are then heaped upon them as bride price or dowry.

This is a proudly orthodox Muslim society in which the *purdah* is strictly enforced; accordingly women wear the *burga* – a heavy cloth mask which conceals the contours of the body from just below the eyes to the waist. Despite this restriction, however, they are by no means shy or timorous creatures, but have forthright and aggressive natures. Wearing their bold dresses layered with jewellery, and surrounded by the aroma of exotic perfumes, they are conspicuous in the desert and the market place.

The Rashaida limit to the absolute minimum their contacts with the Beja groups on whose lands they trespass and whose water rights they abuse. They marry only within their own tribe and rigidly preserve their own ethnic identity.

In the past other groups that have crossed the Red Sea to the Horn have also sought to emphasize and protect their own singularity. In almost every case, with the passage of enough time, they have eventually merged with the peoples already there – adding something of themselves to the dominant cultures in the process. The same can be expected to happen with the Rashaida. They are, after all, merely among the more recent migrants in an interchange of populations that dates back to pre-Christian times and that has continued ever since in both directions and almost without interruption.

The oldest complete skeleton of a human ancestor, 3.2 million years old, was discovered by Dr Donald Johanson in 1974 in the Afar Depression. He nicknamed her "Lucy" after the Beatles song "Lucy in the Sky with Diamonds". The Ethiopians prefer to call her Dinquinesh (Thou Art Wonderful).

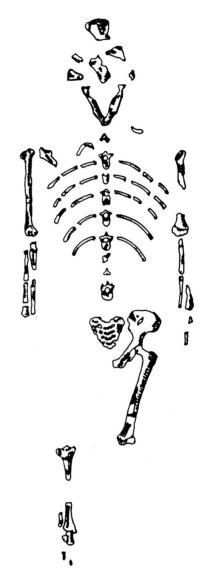

SUCCEEDING PAGES

(82 AND 83): In the inhospitable setting of Lake Abbe, an Afar woman herds her goats.

(84 AND 85): Afar men are traditionally armed with a curved knife, a hardwood staff and, in recent years, a gun. They believe it is better to die than to live without killing.

(86 AND 87): Afar huts are dome-shaped and consist of woven mats and skins stretched over curved armatures of sticks. This form of housing is easily transportable to suit the nomadic life style.

(88 AND 89): Young Afar women are dark eyed and mysterious. The woman on the right sits at the entrance to a *zariba* – an enclosure made of thorny branches to deter predators at night.

Kwosso is the fastest ball game on the African continent, played in the extreme heat of Afar territory in the Rift Valley. *Kwosso* means ball. Light, and usually made of tightly rolled and sewn goatskins, it is the object of fierce competition. Up to two hundred warriors form two different teams. Choosing a leader, each team tries to keep the ball away from the other. The contestants play all day without stopping, finishing only as the sun goes down. Severe injuries and sometimes even deaths may occur.

The *Kwosso* matches are one of the few large-scale social occasions in Afar society that provide the opportunity for young people to strike up romantic relationships.

PRECEDING PAGES, ABOVE AND RIGHT: Virgins go bare-breasted, but after marriage wear a shawl of transparent black cotton called *shash* or *mushal*. This is worn around the head and sometimes draped over the shoulders. Facial scarification is a means of establishing tribal identity as well as enhancing physical beauty.

OVERLEAF: Weekly markets in the foothills above the Rift Valley give the Afar the opportunity to trade rock-salt, *ghee* (clarified butter), camels, cattle and goats, with highland Oromo and Amhara people who bring grain, cloth, and luxury items such as soap, tobacco and beads.

LEFT AND ABOVE: Trading with the Afar at Senbete market, Oromo women are noted for their colourful headcloths and beautifully crafted silver jewellery made from Austrian Maria Theresa dollars, which were used as a trading currency in Ethiopia for many years.

OVERLEAF: Among the nomadic Beja people of Eritrea and of Sudan's Red Sea Hills, the camelherding Beni Amer are renowned for their self-reliant individualism.

ABOVE: This Rashaida man belongs to a Bedouin gypsy tribe which migrated to the Horn of Africa from Saudi Arabia some one hundred and fifty years ago and now lives as desert neighbours of the Beja.

RIGHT: The Beni Amer, a tribe of the Beja people, spend many hours in the quiet of the day recounting stories and exchanging news of their travels and their herds.

OVERLEAF: Beja women from the Tigray and Bilen groups are distinguished by their gold nose rings, the size of which indicates the wealth of their families. Gold jewellery given by her husband at the time of marriage is a woman's security in case of divorce.

RIGHT: Orthodox Muslims, the Rashaida believe that a woman must be veiled. When a woman is married she will wear a heavy jewelled mask that reveals only her eyes. This mask, called the *Arusi*, is decorated with silver and gold and originally came from Saudi Arabia.

ABOVE: After marriage a woman replaces her heavily jewelled mask with a colourful headcloth and a black cloth covering her mouth – worn in memory of the Prophet Mohammed. (It is believed that showing a smile – a sign of happiness – would be disrespectful to the memory of the Prophet.)

PRECEDING PAGES (112 AND 113): Seated Rashaida women wearing the *Arusi* wedding mask.

PRECEDING PAGES (114 AND 115): Worn from the age of five onwards, a heavy cloth mask embroidered with silver threads and beads, called the *burga*, conceals a girl's form from the head to below the waist. It can only be removed in the privacy of the tent. Colourful appliqued skirts, worn in layers and heavily perfumed, like their embroidered masks, are reminders of their recent past in Arabia. Proud of their heritage, the Rashaida repeatedly call out the word "Rashaida" as they dance.

CHAPTER FOUR

EMPIRE OF THE SENSES

The Islamic Coast

n early Pharaonic times, the Horn of Africa – then known lyrically as "God's Land of Punt" – served as an emporium for all the fragrant resins and incense that the High Priests of ancient Egypt required for their rites and mysteries. It is therefore not surprising that the first mention of the region in historical annals is to do with trade. In 2644 BC Pepi II, a Pharaoh of the powerful Vth Dynasty, sent merchant ships down the Red Sea and thence eastwards – along what is now the Gulf of Aden – as far as Cape Gardafui.[1]

Slightly more than one thousand years later the navies of the XVIIIth Dynasty were venturing much further south – certainly to the Benadir coast on which Mogadishu now stands and possibly as far as Lamu and Malindi below the Equator. A commercial expedition commissioned by Queen Hatshepsut in 1450 BC returned from the Horn laden with: "all goodly fragrant woods of God's Land, heaps of myrrh-resin, fresh myrrh trees, ebony, pure ivory, green gold of Amu, cinnamon wood . . . ihmut incense, sonter incense, eye cosmetic, apes, monkeys, dogs, and skins of the southern panther . . ."[2]

By the third century BC the Axumite port of Adulis had emerged as the principal centre for the rich trade of the Horn. Later, after the sack of Adulis in the sixth century AD, other Red Sea towns rose to prominence – among them Massawa and Assab, both of which still survive today amid moderate prosperity.

Many of the mercantile cities of the Somali coast are also very old: Mogadishu, Zeila and Berbera had established themselves as thriving commercial centres by the eighth century AD. Through these gateways, from as far afield as India and China, metals, textiles, cloves, cinnamon, pepper and celadon were brought into the Horn. In return incense, ivory, gold, precious stones, coral, amber, lions, zebras, leopards and ostriches were exported to the Orient.[3]

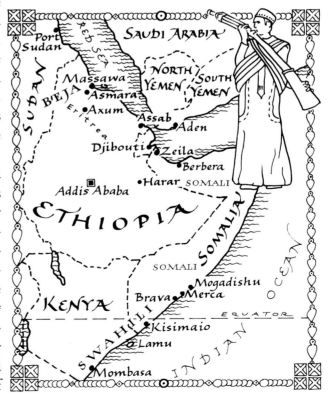

Despite the vast distances that had to be covered, it is clear that links with the Far East were once very strong. A ninth-century Chinese document mentions Berbera, for example, and Sung dynasty pottery (960–1279 AD) has been found along the coast from Mogadishu to Lamu.[4] Moving forward to the fifteenth century, the records of the Ming dynasty tell us that Emperor Yeng Lo received a present of a giraffe from the King of

LEFT: A fishing boat, called *mashua* in Swahili, glides past the island of Lamu.

Malindi in 1415; the strange animal was apparently revered as "holy" by the Chinese who were so impressed that a fleet of junks laden with gifts was dispatched on the hazardous six-month return journey to Africa.[5] Documents from the same period also confirm that Yeng Lo sent a large delegation to Mogadishu in 1422 and note that in 1427 a reciprocal mission was undertaken by an Ambassador from this Somali city.[6]

Today, with more than a million inhabitants, Mogadishu is the Horn's largest coastal settlement. It seems to have enjoyed this pre-eminence for a very long while – the renowned Arab traveller Ibn Battuta visited "Magdashaw" in the second quarter of the fourteenth century and described it as "a town of enormous size."[7] Earlier, Al Yaqubi – an Arab geographer who wrote in the ninth century – mentioned Zeila and Mogadishu as important centres of trade and listed among their exports: "ivory, hides, frankincense and myrrh, slaves, spices and cattle from the hinterlands".[8]

The more things change in the Horn, the more they appear to stay the same. Myrrh and frankincense – which once attracted the interest of the Pharaohs – still remain among the most valuable exports of the Somali coast.

INFLUENCES OF EAST AND WEST

Ancient Egypt still makes its presence felt in modern Somalia. The most popular festival to be held on the coast, *dab-shid* (literally, the lighting of the fire), is celebrated on the day of the solar New Year. This ceremony, in which divine intervention is sought to ensure good crops and the fertility of animals and women, is also called *Eid Fara'un* (the Pharaonic festival) – a folk tradition that echoes the Horn's early contacts.[9]

Among the Oriental influences at work in the Horn, that of the Indian subcontinent is of particular importance: it is not only apparent on the coast but has also filtered into the interior. Thus the dance and music of Somalia and Ethiopia both betray a faint but definite Indian flavour. Several words in the Somali language are borrowed from Hindi and Urdu dialects – including such commonplaces as *miis* (table) and *kursi* (chair). Likewise the clothing worn throughout Somali-speaking areas by both men and women is styled in a manner strongly reminiscent of the subcontinent: the men's *ma'owis* is identical to the *dhoti* of southern India; the women's *qintimo* is a colourful half-sari.

HARAR

Much of the merchandise brought from India to the Somali coast eventually found its way inland. Travellers' tales from the 1850s suggest that, during the trading season, caravans of up to five thousand heavily burdened camels left the port of Berbera *every day*[10] and journeyed west towards the fabled Ethiopian emporium of Harar, a walled Islamic city described by Somalis at the time as "a paradise inhabited by asses".[11]

Despite a somewhat isolated position in the interior, on an eastern branch of the escarpment overlooking the Rift Valley, Harar has probably always had a great deal more in common with the Horn's cosmopolitan coastal culture than with the life of the highlands – and it retains to this day a certain redolence of the Orient. The British adventurer Sir Richard Burton – who, in 1854, was the first European to be allowed to enter the town – disliked the Emir at first sight and later described him as resembling "a little Indian Rajah, an etiolated youth twenty-four or twenty-five years old, plain and thin bearded, with a yellowed complexion, wrinkled brows and protruding eyes".[12]

Many other Europeans were to follow Burton's pioneering footsteps from the coast to Harar. In the late nineteenth century, for example, the French poet Arthur Rimbaud lived in the city, sending complaining letters to his mother, and trading in "silks, cottons, coffee, gum, perfumes, ivory and gold".[13] The strange gothic residence that this eccentric French poet occupied stands to this day – its stained glass windows overlook the market place where shrewd Harari women still offer for sale fine headcloths of Indian muslin and conduct a profitable business in locally made silver, gold and amber jewellery – as well as in beads, baubles and cheap metal trinkets from Bombay and Delhi.

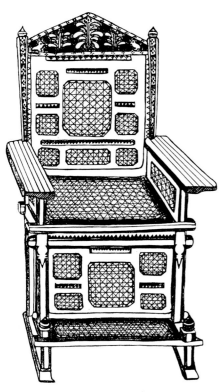

Above: Carved wooden lintel and doorpost from Lamu, Kenya.
Below: Nineteenth century *kiti cha mpingo* "throne" chair made of ebony with inlaid ivory from Lamu town.

With its ninety mosques and shrines, Harar is considered to be the fourth most sacred centre of the Islamic world. It was established in the early sixteenth century by a local chief, Sultan Abu Bakr Muhammad, and was shortly afterwards beseiged and captured by the fanatical Muslim leader Ahmed Gragn – who went on from here to launch a devastating holy war against the Christian Ethiopian highlands.

Gragn was eventually shot dead in 1543 by a musketeer who belonged to an expeditionary force that had been sent by the King of Portugal to assist the Ethiopian Emperor. The force was commanded by the sons of the famous navigator Vasco da Gama – whose galleons had rounded the Cape of Good Hope as early as 1497 and who, in 1502, had established the colony of Mozambique on the East African seaboard.

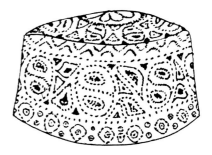

Above: *Kofia* cap embroidered and worn by Swahili men.
Below: Cast bronze *siwa* horn blown on ceremonial occasions from Lamu island.

THE PORTUGUESE

During the sixteenth century, Portuguese flotillas on their way to Goa in western India frequently took shelter in the harbours of the Horn – where several short-lived attempts were made to found additional colonies. By 1593, for example, Mombasa had become the site of a substantial Portuguese garrison quartered in Fort Jesus. A huge structure with crenelated walls almost ten feet thick, the Fort endures to this day – though the flag that flies over it is now that of Kenya.

Also still standing is a lighthouse constructed by Vasco da Gama on the Somali coast at Brava. Here, too, there are a great many imposing old buildings with turrets and battlements in medieval European style. In the absence of clear written records one must trust to local tradition which has it that these strange edifices date back some four hundred years to a period of Portuguese occupation of the town. At that time, apparently, a fleet of ships anchored and sent a delegation ashore requesting land on which to build. The request was at first refused by the Brava elders. However, when the Portuguese captain explained that he only required as much territory as would be "encompassed by an ox-skin", the decision was taken that he should be allowed to go ahead and a document was signed confirming this. The devious captain then acquired the largest hide available and had it carefully cut, spiral fashion, into a thin but continuous strand of leather. This strand was subsequently laid out in a circle that "encompassed a huge area of the best part of Brava" – within which the Portuguese built their enclave.[14]

Though they never succeeded in establishing a proper colony on the southern Somali coast – that job was left to the Italians who arrived three hundred years later – the Portuguese nevertheless did have some impact on the character of the region. Their houses and castles are prominent legacies that contribute tangibly to Brava's enduring grace and charm. In addition, many of the local "Barawani" people are strikingly pale-skinned, with grey and even blue eyes and with straight auburn hair.

Brava's identity, however, has been most profoundly and decisively shaped by yet another influence – the part-Arab, part-Persian Islamic culture, carried for centuries on the dhow sea trade, that links this Somali town closely with many other widely scattered settlements all along the Horn's extensive littoral.

OF DHOWS AND MINARETS. . .

The cultural and religious unity of the Horn's coastal peoples can be traced back to an ancient commerce carried on for the most part by small sailing boats and dhows. Originating in the diverse ports of the Arabian Gulf, the Gulf of Aden and the Red Sea, these flimsy craft have visited East African harbours since time immemorial. Neither has modern shipping technology rendered them redundant. Protected from the heavy Indian Ocean swells by long expanses of coral reef, they still ride the monsoons southward to the Equator from Bandar Abbas, Kuwait, Dubai, Muscat, Mocha and Jeddah.

It was in order to service this dhow trade that pagan Arab and Persian merchants originally established many of the Horn's oldest coastal towns. In consequence, well before the seventh century AD, close links had already been forged between this part of

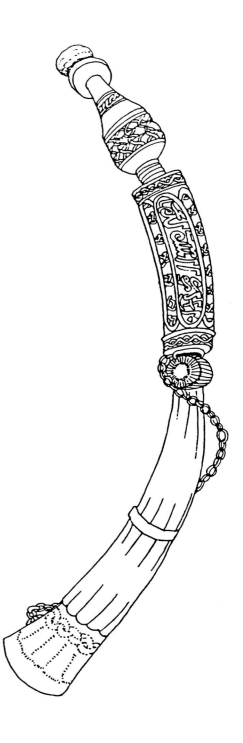

Above and right: Swahili female hand and foot designs painted with henna particularly for celebration and marriage (after *Henna Drawings* by Swabaha Athman Omar Khatib, Lamu, 1986).

Africa and the Middle East. The emergence of the Muslim faith then sealed and confirmed these early connections. Tradition has it that in the year 615 the Prophet advised his followers to flee the Arabian peninsula where they were being persecuted by the powerful Quresh clan. Pointing in the direction of Christian Ethiopia, Mohammed proclaimed: "Yonder lies a country wherein no one is wronged; a land of righteousness. Depart thither and remain until it pleaseth the Lord to open your way before you."

Subsequently, Islamicized Arabs visited the Horn's coastal regions with increasing frequency – and now they came not only to trade but also to seek military conquests, to settle in large numbers and to spread the faith. Sailing in their lean and stately dhows through Bab-el-Mandeb – the narrow "Gate of Tears" that separates the Red Sea from the Gulf of Aden – they rapidly carried the Prophet's message along the Indian Ocean's African edge as far as Dar-es-Salaam, Tanzania's poetically named "Haven of Peace".

In the early days of Muslim settlement, some of the immigrants were very strongly oriented towards the homelands that they had left – and, indeed, some remain so to this day. Others readily merged and intermarried with the Africans, whose cultures they immediately influenced and in due course utterly transformed. This process, however, was by no means all one way: on the contrary, over several centuries, the indigenous peoples had at least an equally profound impact upon the incomers, gradually changing their ideas, their habits and their lifestyles. Coastal society today is thus, above all else, the product of a slow merging of African and Arab worlds – each of which has absorbed elements of the other to create something new.

The best evidence of such synthesis is to be seen in the arts of the coast, which are the products of many different influences. Arab inspiration and Arab techniques may have provided the starting point, but the end results owe much to indigenous talent and ideas (and not a little to the contributions made throughout history by Indian and even by Western visitors). What is remarkable today is the manner in which the differing traits handed down from so eclectic a group of progenitors have successfully combined to produce something strong, individual and distinct – a mongrel by all means, but one with a very pure creative identity that is readily discernible in the woodcarvings, architecture and jewellery of settlements lying thousands of miles apart on the Horn's long seaboard.

HISTORY'S CHILD

Every modern society, it has been said, is the child of its own history. The urbane coastal civilization of the Horn of Africa is no exception to this rule, although it has undoubtedly kept more of its past alive than other more frenetic and aggressive cultures.

Whether in Massawa or Brava, Mogadishu or Lamu, the pace of life today is as unhurried as one imagines it might have been in the Middle Ages. Added to this, the coastal people seem blessed with a special quality of worldly wisdom. Here one encounters a wry but generous tolerance of the carnal frailties of ordinary men and women, an often startling insight into character, and a lithe spirit of compromise. People do not take themselves too seriously and, though they must earn a living, they are not driven by a ferocious work ethic or consumed by neuroses, guilt feelings and nameless dreads. In stark contrast to the pious but often hypocritical preoccupations of the West, concerns about the "human condition" are rarely allowed to become the subject of great angst or of endless philosophical and sociological speculation. Likewise, in a setting where the individual ego can thrive without the need to exploit or humiliate others, ugly and stressful confrontations are rare, and uncomplicated pleasure may be had from the many good things that life has to offer.

Before dawn, all along the coast, the day begins when the muezzin's haunting cry echoes out across silent and deserted streets. Broadcast from the towers of a thousand slender minarets, the beautiful Arabic phrases call the faithful to prayer and reaffirm the greatness, the indivisibility, the mercy and the compassion of God. Mosques here are well attended – even at this hour – and stand at the heart of neighbourhood life. New mosques are constantly built. Sometimes they are the gifts of rich men. More often, however, a community that feels the need of another place of worship will organize a collection to finance the construction costs. Individuals give according to their means and some – carpenters, stone masons, architects – will contribute in kind as well as in cash.

As the sun rises over the eastern ocean, the pre-dawn chill that has shrouded the coast evaporates and the breathless sky lightens from indigo to eggshell blue. The streets are at their busiest between seven and eleven a.m. when legions of sharp-tongued women, their hands and feet fantastically decorated with henna, venture out to haggle with storekeepers and to hunt for bargains in the narrow alleyways of the *souk*. In the Horn of Africa's Red Sea ports, close to Islam's Arabian homeland, the majority of these women are veiled – sometimes from head to foot. On the Somali coast, however, the *yashmak* and *burqa* are almost unknown. Instead a light cotton-voile scarf is drawn decorously across the bridge of the nose – a device that never fails to add enchantment and glamour to the allure of kohl-rimmed almond eyes.

Around midday the open-air markets and colourful bazaars begin to empty out. The heat and humidity become insufferable and all except mad dogs and Englishmen retreat gratefully to the shelter of their homes. Here, in the chattering, companionable lap of the close extended family, a substantial repast is consumed before one and all indulge themselves in the pleasure of the long afternoon siesta.

Repositories of ancient and graceful traditions, some of these houses have remained in the possession of the same family or lineage for as long as a thousand years. In certain districts of Mogadishu, for example, there are buildings that have been handed down, virtually unaltered, through dozens of generations. These two- and three-storied flat-roofed dwellings, with carved and studded wooden doors, decorative rows of niches, and fine plasterwork, huddle together around a warren of narrow streets close to the seafront.

In the towns that line the Red Sea and the Gulf of Aden, stuccoed mud bricks are the most common construction materials, particularly in the poorer quarters. In Mogadishu, Merca, Lamu and other Indian Ocean ports, however, houses are typically built from locally available coral rag stone roofed with mangrove poles and covered with lime mortar.

Whitewashed or pastel-shaded exteriors are everywhere the norm, since these reflect rather than absorb sunlight. In order to allow a free flow of ocean breezes, wide "Moorish" doorways and arched windows are also favoured. Ironically, however, in this gregarious culture, privacy is highly prized: windows thus tend to be fitted with heavy wooden shutters with peepholes through which family members can watch the world going by.

A rather different architectural expression of the same social need is that many of the more prosperous homes are equipped with elaborate exterior balconies above street level. From these, hiding behind the trelliswork, unseen residents secretly delight in spying on the doings of others. Perhaps by way of compensation for the loss of this busybody luxury, single-storey houses are normally built on a square plan around an open courtyard. This device creates a secluded inner space where the women of the family may cook, gossip and do the washing-up out of sight of prying strangers.

Between three and five p.m., as the sun declines in the sky and shadows lengthen, people begin to wake from their siestas. One by one the shops open their doors and the streets fill up again with shoppers and passers-by. In these thronging thoroughfares the timeless and cosmopolitan atmosphere that pervades all the coastal cities seems almost tangible, the aromas of spice and frankincense fill the evening air, and one feels oneself in touch with distant lands and ancient rhythms.

PRECEDING PAGES (124 AND 125): The Islamic religion was introduced into the Horn of Africa by dhow sea traders. The traders also brought their culture, and many towns with a distinctly Arabian flavour grew up along the Red Sea and Indian Ocean coasts.

ABOVE: Islam came to some parts of the coast during the lifetime of the Prophet Mohammed. In the ancient Somali town of Brava, the Mosque of Sheikh Nureini is located where the desert meets the sea.

RIGHT: This traditional Islamic wooden door, carved with floral motifs in Arabic style, is one of many to be seen in the ancient town of Mogadishu, the present day capital of Somalia.

LEFT: A local Swahili man in Lamu blows the *siwa*, a brass horn used to herald ceremonies and religious events. Cast in the lost wax method in the early eighteenth century, it is one of the finest pieces of craftsmanship to be found in the Horn.

LEFT AND ABOVE: A typical interior of a three-storey eighteenth-century coral house on the island of Lamu. The walls feature carved niches, called *zidaka*, in which Swahili women traditionally put their imported Chinese porcelain plates and bowls. The porcelain was believed capable of absorbing evil spirits and was placed in the niches of the back rooms where the most important rituals and life passages took place, including birth and marriage. It was believed that if a plate broke evil had been absorbed in order to protect family members during their most vulnerable times. The variety of the niches helped to decorate the room where women spent many hours every day. In Swahili culture, it was considered a mark of status for women to stay at home and not to go out to work.

LEFT: A Swahili bride, completely veiled from head to toe, sits on her wedding bed awaiting the traditional visit from her husband who will not see her unveiled until their wedding night. The husband (ABOVE) comes to greet her, carrying a small necklace which he places in her hand. A hand-tussle then occurs: whoever ends up holding the necklace is believed to have the upper hand in the marriage.

OVERLEAF: According to the code of orthodox Islam, women must be modest in public. They are required to cover their bodies from head to toe in an all-encompassing black veil called a *bui-bui*. Despite this limitation, they have perfected the art of speaking with their eyes. The Somali woman on the left comes from Brava. The Swahili mother from Lamu (RIGHT), holding her child, reveals elaborate henna decorations on her hand.

Located in Eritrea, the Red Sea port of Massawa has an ancient history stretching back more than a thousand years. First mentioned by the ninth-century Arab Geographer, Al Yaqubi, it was well known to the Portuguese navigators of the early sixteenth century. The port was subsequently seized by the Ottoman Turks, and later still by the Egyptians, whose presence is reflected to this day in the architecture of many mosques and dwellings.

135

ABOVE: By the twelfth century, Islam had spread inland from the Horn's coast. In the Ethiopian interior, the medieval walled city of Harar, with its ninety mosques, is now regarded as the fourth most sacred centre in the Muslim world. Historically, it was renowned as a place of learning and as an emporium of exotic goods. Today a weekly market maintains Harar's reputation as an important trading city and attracts visitors from far and near.

RIGHT: In the port of Massawa, a trellised balcony shows the influence of Turkish Ottoman occupation.

ABOVE: In the Harar market, a basket-seller drives a hard bargain. Finely-made basket work produced in this walled city is highly sought after throughout the Horn.

RIGHT: On her head this woman carries a special basket known as the *agelgil*. It is used for transporting a woman's personal belongings or for carrying *injera* – sour dough pancakes which are the staple food of Ethiopia. Her large amber necklace and intricate silver Koran holder worn over a traditional Harari silk dress are indicative of status and wealth.

The most beautiful female adornment is often seen within the privacy of the houses of Adari families in Harar. On festive occasions, young girls are elaborately decked out in embroidered silks and gold jewellery. Their ornaments and clothing reveal the influence of designs and materials brought in for centuries from Arabia and the Far East. Local craftsmen combine their own inspirations with these imports.

OVERLEAF: Muslim Afar girls from the family of the Sultan of Tadjourah in the Djibouti Republic wear some of the most exotic gold jewellery to be found in the Horn. Some of the jewellery is locally made and some is brought in by relatives returning from Saudi Arabia, Yemen, Pakistan and India. The greatest finery is called for during marriages and other celebrations.

GAUNT AND LEOPARD-COLOURED LANDS

Somali Nomads of the Ogaden Desert

ehind the great cities that edge the maritime plains of the Horn of Africa lies a land of savannahs and semi-desert. Fissured and split with deep gullies – along which roaring flash floods descend in the rainy seasons – this austere country is strewn with the weird totems of termite chimneys and dotted with ancient mountain ranges.

One of the first Westerners to explore this strange terrain was the nineteenth-century English adventurer Sir Richard Burton. He was intrigued by the tribesmen he found living here – Somali bedouins of "most susceptible character, and withal uncommonly hard to please. . ." On several occasions he commented on their love of fighting, describing them as "by no means deficient in the wily valour of wild men. . . When the passions of rival tribes are violently excited they will use with asperity the dagger and spear. . . Their massacres are fearful."[1]

KITH AND KIN

Though some groups have been settled for centuries in cities like Mogadishu and Berbera, and though there are growing numbers of farmers, the Somali remain in essence a hard and warlike nomadic race. They have changed surprisingly little since Burton first encountered them: even today almost half of all the people of the Somali Republic are still committed pastoralists. Proud and aloof, stubborn and conservative, they follow the ways of their fathers – ways that have been tested and proved by time.

As a "nation" in the modern sense, the Somalis are almost unique in Africa: they speak only one language – Somali; they are further united by their common nomadic heritage which gives a remarkable degree of consistency to their culture; and, last but by no means of least, they share a single religion – Islam.

Despite these common factors, another influence is also at work – one that tends towards conflict and feud. This is a culture in which blood is indeed thicker than water and in which patrilineal kinship still forms the basis of almost all relationships. Lacking ties to any specific place, the only means by which the individual can locate himself in society is in terms of his lineage – through knowledge of which he establishes not only

LEFT: Somali camel herder from the Ogaden.

the links that bind him to his kin, but also the varying degrees of distance that separate him from unrelated others.

LEARNING IN A HARD SCHOOL

In traditional Somali society it was a simple fact of life that if new pastures *could* be occupied by force of arms then they *would* be occupied; conversely if territory that one tribe had made its own by customary usage could not be defended, then others would certainly encroach on it. Running through the entire culture, even today, is a firm belief that might is right: in all circumstances, the strong win and the weak lose.

Since small groups are vulnerable groups, the normal pattern of Somali nomadism is one in which several families gather together into a sort of "hamlet on the move", the members of which then share the all-important tasks of defence and animal husbandry. A distinction is maintained between individual and group interests, but it is also recognized that the individual only survives because of his membership of the group.

Camels are the nomads' most precious assets. They represent a vital source of milk and meat on the hoof, they are the carriers of burdens, and they are symbols of the prosperity and self-reliance of the tribe. Surprisingly, however, their care is entrusted entirely to boys and young men who, from the age of seven onwards, lead a life of Spartan toughness. They rarely have a roof of any kind over their heads and they sleep out under the stars on thin mats, protected from the cold of the desert nights only by the clothes they wear. From such experiences and from their elders the camel boys quickly acquire all the skills and values that will stand them in good stead in later life. They learn which are the best pastures and which grasses can endanger their stock; they learn basic veterinary procedures; they learn how to manage the herds and to love and care for the individual animals in their charge;[2] most important of all, in a land that has only two perennial rivers, they learn where to find water.

Unlike the rangelands – which are seen as a gift of God to be occupied but not owned by man – wells are indisputably the property of the particular lineages that have invested time and energy in developing them. In Ethiopia's Ogaden region (so named after the Somali clan that inhabits it[3]) there are some wells that are thought to have been in constant use for more than two thousand years and that continue today to be the focus of large gatherings of nomads.

Around the wells, during periods of scarcity, competition for water can become intense; in consequence, strife and drought frequently occur together. Somalis contrast such conditions longingly with the rarer and more desirable occasions when peace prevails and milk is plentiful. Nevertheless there is a great willingness to go to war. The camel camps easily transform themselves into effective fighting units characterized by high morale and strong group identity and putting to devastating use the discipline and endurance skills of their members.

Every nomadic Somali boy is born into what is known as a "dia-paying group". These institutions – which may have as few as one hundred or as many as one thousand members – consist in each case of a number of shallow lineages reckoning their descent through no more than eight generations to a common founder. Such groups often form the basis of raiding parties and are as important as the camel camps in promoting discipline and camaraderie. Their specific function, however, is to pay any blood debts that may be incurred by their individual members.

Nomads traditionally value a man's life at 100 camels: if a disastrous feud is to be avoided after a killing, 100 camels must be paid to the lineage of the victim. Since few men are rich enough actually to own 100 camels – or even anything like that number – it follows that some sort of insurance scheme is required to settle the debt. This, in essence, is the job of the dia-paying group.

Wrongs once committed are rarely forgiven and, unless the account is cleared, tend to become the sources of long-term grievances. If compensation is refused the dia-

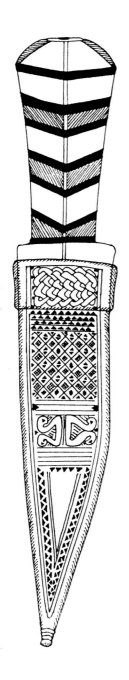

Somali dagger, *tooray*.

paying group of the injured party will frequently seek to extract it by force – or, alternatively, to redress the perceived "wrong" by killing a member of the perpetrator's own lineage. This, coupled with the ever-pervasive competition for scarce resources that is the fundamental dimension of nomadic Somali life, explains why a quarrel between two individuals can quickly and easily escalate into a full-scale battle between their dia-paying groups. Such engagements, in their turn, then tend to draw in other more distantly-related lineages in a widening spiral of violence that culminates eventually in generalized clan enmity.

Great delight, it may be added, is taken in this process by young men of fighting age – who taunt one another with impromptu poems and songs calculated to rub the salt of insult into wounds already inflicted.

A LANGUAGE FOR WAR AND LOVE

Sir Richard Burton, the first foreigner to take a genuine interest in the Somali people, found that they had "thousands of songs, some local, others general, upon all conceivable subjects". He added: "It is strange that a dialect which has no written character should so abound in poetry and eloquence," and concluded: "The country teems with poets, poetasters, poetitos, poetaccios. . . every man has his recognized position in literature as accurately defined as though he had been reviewed in a century of magazines – the fine ear of this people causing them to take the greatest pleasure in harmonious sounds and poetical expressions, whereas a false quantity or a prosaic phrase excite their violent indignation. . ."[4]

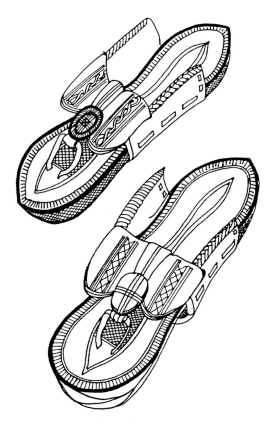

Above: Somali leather sandals, *kabo*.
Below: Wooden camel bell, *koor*.

Closely related to the Afar and Oromo tongues, Somali is by far the most widespread of the Horn's Hamitic languages; it is also the most expressive and lends itself well to the emotive eloquence of war.

One man who knew this was Sayid Mohamed Abdullah Hassan – who united the Somali people in the early years of this century in a bitter fight against colonial encroachment. His remarkable success in winning hearts and minds is partly attributable to his valour, but of at least equal importance was his inspiring oratory. This was mainly reserved for exhorting his own forces, but occasionally he would also give the enemy a taste of his rhetoric. "I have no forts, no houses," he once wrote to the British commander in northern Somalia:

> I have no cultivated fields, no silver or gold
>   for you to take . . . The country is bush . . .
> If you want wood and stone, you can get them in plenty.
> There are also many termite hills.
> The sun is very hot.
> All you can get from me is war . . .
> If you want peace, go away from my country . . .

The British dubbed Sayid Mohamed "The Mad Mullah". However, in twenty years of war several thousand colonial troops lost their lives in the many battles fought against him and the cost to the British taxpayer was estimated to have exceeded £5,000,000.

A nationalist born before his time, a fierce and ruthless fighter, a warlord cast in the classic mould, Sayid Mohamed also had his softer and gentler moments:

> For you I shall put saddles on long-rumped bay horses
> For you I shall pour many camels into the empty and
>   desolate corrals;
> You will drink your fill of the milk of milch cows
>   which have given birth,
> You will fall upon the vessels of sour milk as camels
>   fall upon the water . . .

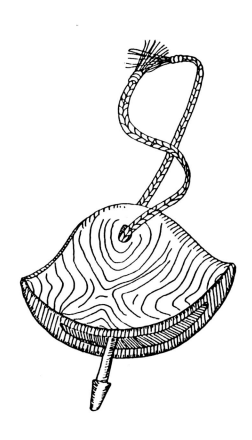

147

At the time that they were composed, the Sayid's poems were never written down. The only reason that they are still in existence is because of the highly effective tradition of "oral literature" on which Sir Richard Burton commented. This tradition, furthermore, had its own form of copyright law – anyone who memorized someone else's poem and wanted to recite it at some later date was under a strict obligation to remember the text accurately and to reproduce it faithfully because: "he was considered to be the channel of communication and in no way a co-author with the original poet . . ." The reciter also "had to give the name of the poet at each recital, and its omission or a knowing misappropriation was treated as a serious breach of the ethical code."[5]

Until very recently Somali was an unwritten language – so such word-of-mouth transmission was the *only* mechanism by which songs and poetry could be preserved. In 1972, however, a script was finally devised – an event that almost immediately prompted an amazing efflorescence of poems in book form. This remarkable publishing explosion has continued ever since. Focused almost entirely on love poetry, it has proved to be a major stimulus to literacy.

Now modern and traditional poems are finding their way into print. For example:

> The home we have set up, the bed I have spread for you,
> The trust between us, our resolve and the oath;
> If you have turned away from all these and abandoned me
>   in a deserted place
> Then it was sheer folly that possessed me.[6]

Or, equally powerful:

> I bade you farewell, wished you a journey full of blessing;
> Every hour you exist, when you go to sleep and when you awake
> Keep in mind the troth between us
> I am waiting for you. Come safely back, come safely back.[7]

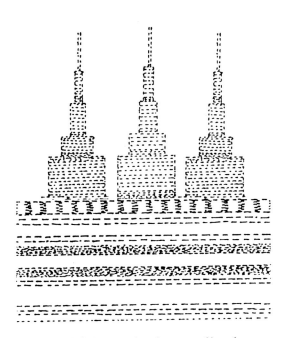

Above and right: Border designs of hand-woven cotton cloth called *alindi* worn by Somali men.

Such evocative and sentimental verses are indicative of an intriguing irony: although they are a hard-edged and pragmatic pastoral people, the Somalis are also great romantics and this surprising vein of tenderness is coupled with a gentle and imaginative appreciation of the beauty of the natural world.

Under the great curve of the sky, where the nomads wander on the limitless prairies, there is poetry in the air from morning to night: in the kraal at dawn, the hollow clunk of the camel bells as the milking begins; at noon, the bleat of goats carried far across the gaunt and leopard-coloured grasslands on the rustling wings of a dry summer breeze; towards evening the haunting, urgent whistle of the camel boy as he guides his grumbling herds through the bush to the home pens.

Soon after sunset a beautiful planet appears in the heavens, signalling the hour at which the sheep must be driven into the thorn enclosures where they will spend the night. Western people call that planet Venus, and associate it with love; for the nomads, however, it is *maqal hidhid* – from *maqal* (meaning lambs) and *hid* (meaning to shut in).

Then darkness envelops the earth – a darkness made luminous by the phosphorescent nightlights of the Milky Way and by the ever-changing disk of the moon. Now, across the lonely savannahs, from *zariba* to *zariba*, echo out the voices of the Bedouin girls – voices that are soft, low and plaintive, "rather like music than mere utterance".[8]

Such evening conversations are at their most relaxed in the rainy seasons when the rangelands are green and the milking camels are productive. This is the best of times in the pastoral cycle; to celebrate it the camel herders will, if possible, pen their stock near to the larger family camps so that, under cover of darkness, they may serenade the virgins within. Extempore dances frequently occur – usually with the boys and girls facing each other in two rows that bashfully approach and recede, approach and recede. Occasionally the boys will jump high into the air – a kind of stiff, vertical leap that shows them to be strong and graceful, swift and sure, and thus made of warrior stuff.

It is during the rainy seasons, too, that marriage proposals are most often made. Temporarily relieved of the heavy responsibilities that rest on their shoulders at other times of the year, eligible young men walk from hamlet to hamlet to search for unwedded girls. They will frequently sing to them and, if the performance is good enough, romance may blossom.

Much traditional poetry focuses on the plight of sweethearts who come from rival or warring tribes. The underlying lyricism in nomadic culture, however, is by no means confined to the themes of love and war. A great many songs and proverbs also extoll the virtues of the pastoral lifestyle itself, often comparing it favourably with the miserable existence of the settled farmer. Some verses are distinguished by an austere beauty, managing to say much in a very few words about the essential realities of the pastoral existence. Of drought, for example, the nomadic bard observes that:

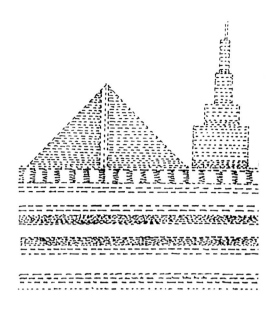

> Wherever one looks, the life of this world depends on water
> But if the water itself feels thirsty,
> From what well can one quench its thirst?[9]

The muse that inspires Somali nomads even shapes their prayers and blessings: "In the midst of sweet abundance, and in time of pestilence, all hail, God who watches us." Or: "Of the two ways, that which is right; of the two decisions, that which is good – may just God lead you to follow." Or simply: "May God make milk for you."

A DESERT FAITH

In its origins an uncluttered and austere desert faith, Islam is the religion of all Somalis. It first came here a very long time ago – almost certainly during the lifetime of the Prophet Mohammed himself. Brought inland from the coast by immigrant Arab *sheikhs*, it rose rapidly to prominence. Its great and immediate success, however, probably owed less to the fiery zeal of its proselytizers than to the essential tolerance of the Message that they carried – a Message that has never sought to crush the indigenous cultures that have received it, but rather to adapt to their spiritual needs. Because of this flexibility it is still possible to detect within Somali Islam the continued presence of certain pagan beliefs and practices that have survived more than a thousand years of monotheism.

As one journeys beyond Somali country, further into the deep interior of the Horn, the pagan substratum of religious life moves ever nearer to the surface. Westward from the red plains of the Ogaden the countryside begins to ascend steeply through foothills planted with stands of euphorbia cactus, which in their turn give way to vast and mossy mountain ranges shrouded in mist and cold. In this eerie and ancient setting, as we shall see in the next chapter, superstition and magical beliefs dominate human consciousness and Islam walks hand in hand with the worship of older gods.

SUCCEEDING PAGES
(150 AND 151): The savannahs of Somalia and Ethiopia, which are home to millions of Somali nomads, are thought to support almost one half of the world's population of single-humped camels. Where the terrain permits, cattle are also herded.

(152 AND 153): Somali nomads depend on the camel for transport of both their possessions and portable homes. The long curved branches carried by the camels are used as the main structural supports for the bee-hive-shaped huts (*aqal*).

(154 AND 155): Camels are essential in this semi-desert environment as water holes and wells are far apart. During the rainy season, newly formed ponds are an extra source of water but, throughout most of the year, herders must rely on traditional wells.

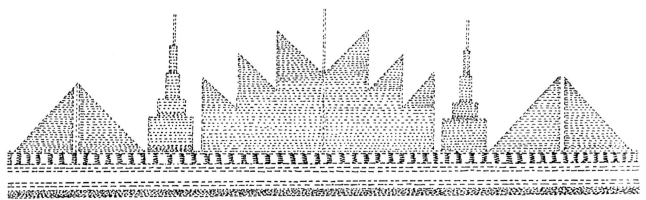

Many well sites in the Ogaden (which straddles the border between Somalia and Ethiopia) have been in use for up to two thousand years according to recent carbon dating of camel dung. There is such a great demand for water that the nomads follow specific rules as to times and sites for watering their herds.

LEFT: In the Ogaden women and children are left in charge of herding goats. RIGHT: A Somali nomad girl husks millet, which will be used to complement her family's staple diet of camel milk.

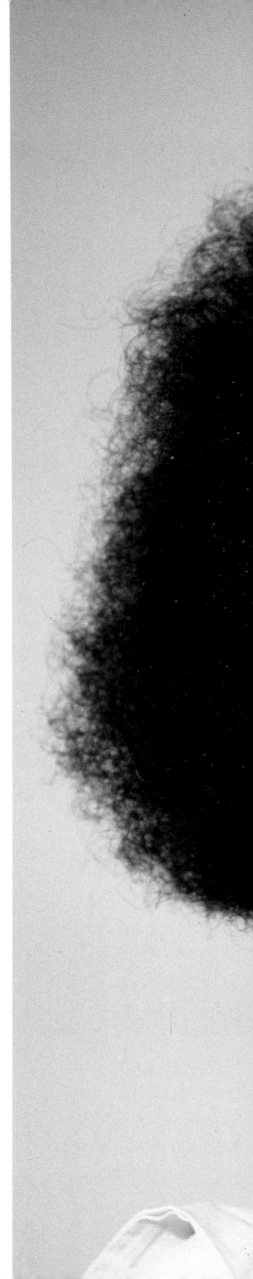

Pride, endurance, grace and physical beauty characterize the Somali people. Nomads regard themselves as being of noble descent. The great clan families claim patrician Arab founders whose blood lines go back as far as Prophet Mohammed himself. Despite the Muslim tradition, the women go unveiled, proud and free. They show great independence of mind and action, qualities which stem from the pastoral lifestyle.

Market days in the Ogaden create a colourful kaleidoscope of people and merchandise. Women wearing beautiful headwraps, either locally made or imported from India, arrive at the weekly market carrying goods for exchange, either on their heads or on the backs of donkeys. The large marrow (ABOVE) is one of the few vegetables that can be grown in the arid region of the Ogaden.

LEFT: From the Indian Ocean to the Somali-Ethiopian interior, nomadic festivities always include dance and song. After the rains, when milking cows are productive and the nomads are most relaxed, camel herders serenade eligible girls and impromptu dances in many different styles frequently occur. In the hinterland, women perform seductive dances using veils to the accompaniment of female drummers.

SUCCEEDING PAGES
(166 AND 167, 168 AND 169): On the coast, bright voluminous robes and vigorous hand-clapping heighten the swirling movements of the dancers.

(170 AND 171, 172 AND 173): In the Ogaden, men and women frequently dance together, facing each other in two rows. At first the men bashfully approach the women and then draw back. As the dance builds in momentum the men begin to jump high in the air showing the strength, grace and swiftness characteristic of a brave warrior.

CHAPTER SIX

SPIRIT WORLDS

The Oromo Pilgrimage to Sheikh Hussein and to the Caves of Sof Omar

 ll three of the great monotheistic religions originated in the Middle East; all three in their early years crossed the Red Sea and established bridgeheads in the Horn. Judaism, the faith of the Falashas, was never strongly evangelistic. Christianity and Islam, on the other hand, sought converts from the beginning. Like the vanguards of armies on the move, the missionaries of these latter two faiths established themselves in new territory whenever and wherever this proved possible. The result, today, is that the region's older, pagan beliefs appear almost everywhere to have been vanquished: if they survive at all in their original form, then they do so only in remote and threatened enclaves.

Conversion is a process, however, not a sudden shift from one state of being to another. Thus in some areas it is still possible to find large numbers of people whose beliefs are in a state of transition, whose concepts of God and of the spiritual realm seem to change shape from day to day, like the colourful patterns of a kaleidoscope.

This is particularly true of the Oromo, a great and extensive Hamitic race of pastoralists and farmers. Also known as the Galla – a name that they themselves despise – they number perhaps twenty million and are the largest single ethnic group in the Horn.

Though most Oromos are today at least nominally Muslims or Christians (depending very much on where they live), many still keep a place in their hearts for a different god, *Waq*, who is the sky, whose blessing is the rain, whose girdle is the rainbow. He manifests himself through countless spirits and several lesser divinities, but he is also envisaged as being single, mysterious and tremendous – the Most High. Thus it is said: "*Waq* is one; man is many. *Waq* has no equals. He is above all things. Nothing is above him."[1]

Such notions are by no means entirely incompatible with the teachings of the monotheistic faiths, but nevertheless have been sharply discouraged by the mullahs and the priests. Oromo elders see the results of this and say: "From generation to generation our people move further away from *Waq*." They believe it is no accident that the earth is drying up and that good health, fertility, and material wellbeing have all been diminished: "Oh *Waq*," they pray, "have mercy on us. Oh earth have mercy on us. Oh *Waq* give us rain."[2]

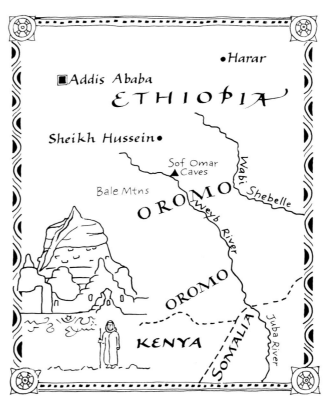

LEFT: Pilgrim on on his way to pay homage to Sheikh Hussein.

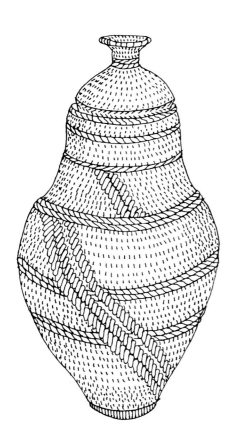

Above and right: Oromo baskets made of tightly woven grass.

MIGRATION AND SEPARATION

Had they possessed a coherent identity capable of binding them into a politically effective unit, then the Oromo would undoubtedly have emerged as a force to be reckoned with in modern times. The history of this people has, however, been one of constant division and subdivision into different clans – such as the Borana, the Guji, the Arsi, the Ittu and the Mecha. Despite common traditions of origin, and a common language, these and all other Oromo sections are now fractured and alienated from one another – a state of affairs that is further complicated by their wide geographical distribution in many parts of Ethiopia.

It has not always been so. At one time the Oromo were a single tribe living in the northeastern part of the Horn, in what is now the Somali Republic. Specialized cattle herders, they were much more susceptible to the desertification that is known to have affected this area than were the camel- and goat-herding Somalis – and thus were gradually driven out as droughts became more and more common. What seems to have happened is that whenever the Oromos vacated arid pastures, opportunistic groups of Somali nomads, with their hardier animals, simply moved in behind them to fill the gap. Relative fighting skills were probably not a significant factor in this process of displacement; indeed, in terms of numbers and military strength, it is likely that the retreating Oromos were more than a match for the advancing Somalis.

What is certain is that the refugee tribesmen proved themselves to be fierce and effective warriors from the moment that they first entered Ethiopia in the late fifteenth century. The route of their migration seems first to have taken them south into Kenya, then west towards Lake Turkana, and finally northward again along the floor of the Rift Valley in a massive and very rapid advance towards the centre of old Abyssinia.

For a considerable period, none of the indigenous peoples were able to withstand them. As a result, by the mid-sixteenth century, some Oromo bands had reached the frontiers of Tigray.

CYCLES OF LIFE AND DEATH

The migrants' remarkable military successes owed much to the manner in which their society was organized into age sets – including a highly motivated warrior grade.

Known as *gada*, this complex system of stratification survives today in its original form among the Borana of Sidamo province and, to a lesser extent, among the neighbouring Guji. Elsewhere it is in steep decline but nevertheless continues to exert a powerful subliminal influence on many aspects of Oromo culture and religion.

Each *gada* class – known by the Oromo term *luba* – consists of all the sons, of whatever age, born to the fathers of another specified class. It is the members of this *luba* who must move together through the eleven grades that will take them from birth to retirement. In the first grade they are treated like girls – even down to their style of dress. In the second grade they are given proper male names and are entrusted with looking after calves and horses. In the third grade they are assigned as the guardians of the family herds. In the fourth grade they must study military tactics and participate in raiding expeditions. At the end of the fifth grade, after *forty years* have passed, they at last earn the right to father children of their own. The most important transition, however, does not come until the forty-eighth year of the cycle – when, in a mass ceremony, all the members of the *luba* are circumcised and initiated as the new ruling elite of the tribe.

The military role of the *gada* system was clear enough in the sixteenth century when Oromo age regiments rampaged across the Abyssinian countryside according to a strict and repetitive calendar. Every eight years as a new class acquired warrior status, it would set out to prove itself by extending the frontiers of the tribe and by slaughtering all who attempted to block the path of its advance.

Even in those days, however, there was much more to age grading than a mere organizational principle that facilitated warfare. The system also created the social framework through which individuals were enabled to express their devotion to *Waq* – the sky god who, as the bringer of rain and the source of all life, would sometimes come down in the cool of the evening to walk and to talk with mortal men.

There was a need for ritual experts who could meet this deity face to face. The *gada* filled that need with a range of hereditary and elective priestly offices and, at the same time, linked every class member with his own powerful ancestors in the spirit world.

Though subsequently adulterated by Christian and Islamic thinking, it is these devotional aspects of the *gada* system (rather than the military ones) that have survived most strongly into modern times. Indeed, they still form the bedrock of the Oromos' curiously "oriental" world view. An epicyclical calendar is used to calculate the mystical influence of history on the present course of events: "The experience of a particular ancestral *gada* class – calculated through an epicyclical historical calendar as one that was in power thirty-five *gada* periods, or two hundred and eighty years, earlier – is believed to have a determining influence, a *dachi*, upon the fate of its latter-day successor. The class currently in power is obliged to avoid the chief misfortunes which befell its ancestors and to repeat the outstanding successes. At the same time it is setting a precedent which will affect its descendants thirty-six *gada* generations in the future."[3]

SACRED PLACES

This concept of an endless succession of lives inextricably bound up with one another contains clear elements of ancestor worship that are easily identified in the religious practises of many sections of the Oromo today. Furthermore, the notion that man's destiny is shaped by a pervasive mystical influence from the past is extended beyond the ancestor category in Oromo religion to incorporate a realm of non-human spirits known as *ayana*. These are not detached, incorporeal beings floating around in the ether; rather they are seen as being closely tied to specific aspects of the everyday world. Thus mountains, caves, springs, running water, snakes, trees and certain other natural features are believed to possess particularly strong *ayanas* which can act as intermediaries between man and *Waq*. As one tribal elder puts it: "We see the *ayanas* as flowing from *Waq*, filling the whole of creation, filling every creature, making things the way they are . . . It is in many, many *ayanas* that *Waq* himself comes close to us and that we are united to him."

The importance of such beliefs to the Oromo is expressed by the sacrifices that the *gada* class in power is obliged to make at certain times of the year to the *ayanas* and to *Waq*. Associated with a number of sacred shrines, such ritual occasions have traditionally been the focus of massive pilgrimages from all parts of Ethiopia. During the twentieth century, however, successive governments have sought to put a stop to these popular seasonal migrations, which have been seen as containing the dangerous seeds of possible Oromo reunification.

As a result, only one of the pilgrimages still survives today on a scale that is in any way representative of the old traditions. This survival, furthermore, has been achieved by a long process of compromise with Islam that has produced a bizarre amalgam combining elements of a Muslim saint cult with a continuing reverence for *Waq* and for the *ayanas*. The focus of this pilgrimage is the tomb of Sheikh Hussein – possibly the first Islamic missionary ever to leave the relative safety of the coast and to penetrate deep into the heart of Ethiopia.

In the province of Bale, cut off from the main body of the central escarpment by the Rift Valley's deep furrow, an isolated arm of mountain country gives birth to the Wabi Shebelle, which then meanders eastward across the Somali plains. Seven centuries ago Sheikh Hussein followed this river from its mouth on the Indian Ocean to its headwaters. Since Christianity had not succeeded in crossing the Rift, he found himself surrounded only by savage and susceptible pagans among whom he then happily spent the rest of his days performing miracles and preaching the word of God.

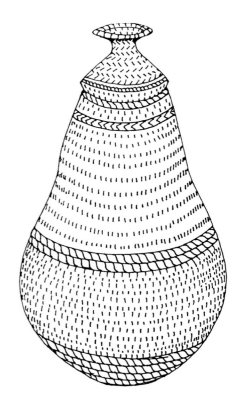

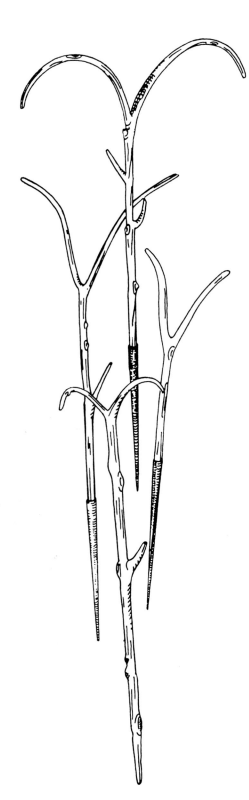

Forked walking sticks, known as *Oule Sheikh Hussein*, carried by all pilgrims.

When the vanguard Oromo age regiments arrived in Bale in the early sixteenth century Sheikh Hussein had been dead, buried and canonized as a Sufi saint for some three hundred years. Hearing of his great works, however, and of the miraculous powers of his spirit, the invaders wisely assimilated him into their own complex belief system. Each February, on the anniversary of his death, more and more of them would join with the Muslim pilgrims who congregated to honour his shrine.

During the same period, the Oromos who settled in Bale also established a place of pilgrimage more directly related to their own faith on a nearby mountain peak. Here, from within a cave inhabited by enormous serpents, a cult figure known as the *Abba Muda* dispensed ritual benedictions to his pagan devotees. This "father of annointing" (the literal translation of his name) smeared the head of each pilgrim with butter and blessed him with the words: "May the milk of your herds flow in abundance. May you be loaded with goods. May your favourite cow's udder be full of milk from which none drinks but he who has received Unction. It is the wish of my heart that you should prosper. May *Waq* be with you. May he accept your sacrifices."[4]

Because it became immensely popular and focused the potentially warlike energies of tens of thousands of Oromos from near and distant provinces, the pilgrimage to the *Abba Muda* was permanently banned in the early years of the twentieth century by the government of Imperial Ethiopia. The parallel pilgrimage to the Islamic shrine of Sheikh Hussein, however, was allowed to continue. Today, the identities of Sheikh Hussein and the *Abba Muda* have merged in many people's minds. So too, albeit at a higher level, have *Waq* and Allah become one and the same.

No serious contradiction or schizophrenia is involved. Rooted in the very deepest soil of the human psyche, the urge to visit sacred places transcends sectarian differences. As an Oromo elder explained: "Our people go on pilgrimage to Bale; the pagans say they go to the Abba Muda; the Muslims say they go to Sheikh Hussein."[5] But both, in reality, are going to the same place – and in order to find the same spiritual consolation.

THE ECSTASY OF FAITH

In the past, according to the legends, *Waq* lay with his belly close to the whole of the earth, "fertilizing it with his rain".

It is easy to see why simple rural folk should believe that the pagan deity still does this in Bale, and to understand why, though nominally Muslims, they also continue to offer sacrifices to the ever-present sky to ensure the wellbeing of their tribes, the fertility of their women, and the uninterrupted bounty of their harvests. This, above all else, is a mysterious land, imbued with a deep aura of the numinous – a land of low-hanging clouds and of soaring peaks carpeted with groves of ancient juniper upon which cold mists and fogs can suddenly descend.

Here, too, amidst the mighty *ayanas* of the mountain springs, the limestone caverns and the trees, the notion that the spirit of a Muslim saint should still be capable of performing miracles is by no means out of place. In all things one senses the undeniable presence of the supernatural and of the unexplained – and it is perhaps only in such an awe-inspiring context that the phenomenon of the pilgrimage to the shrine of Sheikh Hussein could possibly make any kind of sense.

More than just a pilgrimage in fact, what we have here is an institution resonant with archaic and near-forgotten rhythms, an institution that stretches out its arms to the farthest reaches of the Horn and that draws in the nomad, the smallholder and the villager alike, making vagabonds of them all. They come in groups a hundred and two hundred strong, from north and south, from east and west – great bands of shabby men, ragged women, threadbare children – all impelled here, magnetized, pulled along by the compulsive ecstasy of their faith.

The wayfarers carry curious forked staves known as *Oule Sheikh Hussein*. These have a variety of functions in addition to their obvious role as walking sticks. They serve, for example, as props for the devout to lean on during the communal prayers which are always undertaken standing up and which, though now heavily Islamicized, are still often followed by a sacrificial meal – a portion of which is offered to *Waq*.[6]

Over and above such pragmatic uses, the forked sticks also have symbolic significance: an unwritten folk law, dating back to the days of the great *Abba Muda* rituals, requires villagers to give hospitality to anyone displaying the pilgrims' regalia – of which the *Oule Sheikh Hussein* are the most important part. In the process of jumping the gap between paganism and Islamic saint cult, the sticks, although now made simply of wood, have maintained the distinctive shape that was originally given to them by tips of curved antelope horn.[7]

Other aspects of the *Abba Muda* rites have also been carried over into the cult of Sheikh Hussein. Once they have started on the road, for example, pilgrims must abstain from sexual intercourse, must not cut their fingernails or their hair, and may never sleep indoors. A wild and unkempt appearance is thus characteristic of the wandering bands of supplicants, particularly since many of their members, whose homes are in distant provinces, will have been obliged to journey overland on foot, or on the backs of mules or donkeys, for as long as six months.

Poverty is an additional reason for the extreme dishevelment of some of the wayfarers. The Horn of Africa is, after all, one of the poorest regions of the world's poorest continent. In such a context it is easy to understand why the Sheikh Hussein pilgrimage – with its customary hospitality – has also become a complete way of life for legions of the landless, the unemployed and the dispossessed.

Midway between the peaks and the plains, in the eastern foothills of the Bale mountain range, the mosque and shrine of Sheikh Hussein, together with the small town of the same name, lie at the heart of a substantial sacred zone. Here, no trees may be felled and – out of further deference to powerful arboreal *ayanas* – pilgrims hang strips of animal skin, strings of rags and sometimes even bunches of hair on certain branches.

Such offerings, intended to keep the spirits mindful of the devotees and their requests, are not the only features of traditional Oromo religion encountered in this supposedly Islamic place. The old serpent cult of the *Abba Muda*, for example, rears its head in the stipulation that every pilgrim must visit the so-called "grotto of the snake" – there to burn incense before a weirdly sinuous formation etched out of the rock by dripping water. Other objects in the grotto – which is reached by a pathway flanked by various venerated symbols – include a petrified figure thought to resemble a nude woman in the act of combing her hair and a group of horsemen said to have been turned to stone by Sheikh Hussein himself when they tried to invade the area.

Nearby there is the "honey grotto" where water – symbolizing the honey that was once made for the Sheikh by his bees – trickles down from a black rock. Other wonders include a precipice that miraculously opened up to engulf a trespassing sinner and, to the southeast of the town, a small mountain said to have been piled up by the saint during the course of a single night.

The mausoleum of the Sheikh, upon which all the travellers ultimately focus their energies, stands at the centre of a spacious walled compound beneath a gleaming white-washed cupola thirty feet high. The crypt itself is reached through a narrow doorway so low that supplicants are obliged to stoop or crawl to gain entrance. They do so willingly, with an expressed urgency and devotion – for this is a blessed place.

Here, on sacred ground, pagan and Islamic ideas combine to create a potent religious synergy. On the one hand the Oromo concept of a close and influential spirit world allows devotees to draw down miracles from the very walls of the tomb – for though the body of the saint may be dead, it is undoubtedly the case that his *ayana* lives on in his burial place. In a similar fashion, Muslim thought enshrines the notion of *baraka*, a special quality of luck, charisma and leadership bestowed by God on particular individuals who may then act as channels to the supernatural – a quality that remains

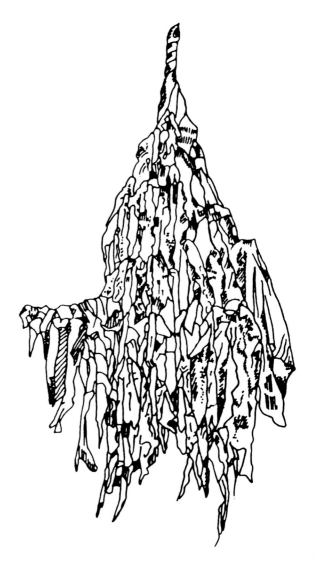

Torn strips of cloth and hide given as votive offerings after prayers have been answered by the spirit of Sof Omar.

179

even after the individual who was granted it has passed away.[8]

The pilgrims are thus confronted by a double opportunity as they stoop to enter the crypt: not only may they petition the *ayana* of Sheikh Hussein; also, they may reasonably expect to imbibe some portion of his remarkable *baraka*. It is thus with the greatest possible fervour that they seek here the remedy for all their ills, the consolation for all their griefs, and the solution to all their problems.

The dark, still air of the tomb is charged with the body heat of the devotees who crowd in. Some circle the floor, praying, crying, chanting. Others, seemingly consumed by a transcendental passion, writhe and throw themselves about. Others still, half concealed in corners, in nooks and crannies, sit slumped, spellbound and oblivious, as though the narcotic of holiness has plunged them into a fugue from which they may never awake . . . Here a teenage girl raises her skirts and pushes between her legs a handful of white powder scraped from the walls; there a group of women rub more of the saintly dust into their ears and noses, across their faces and breasts, and onto their hair . . . Here a man kisses and caresses the bare, chalky stone as if it were his lover; there a bearded patriarch spits into a little pile of dust he has collected in his palm, makes a paste, eats some, smears the remainder on his forehead . . .

Outside the tomb, the dominant spirit of Sheikh Hussein can still be felt – guiding and directing the gliding feet of countless devotees who press themselves against the exterior walls with moans of rapture. And even beyond the precincts of the compound, the same mood bewitches and inspires a crowd of wild-eyed men and boys who have gathered to intone the praises of the saint – a litany known as *Baro* that owes nothing to Islam. In a custom that resonates with the ancient ways of the rain god, there is at first much spitting on the ground – not an insult among the Oromo (who speak of a dead person as having "grown dry") but rather a traditional blessing. Then, one after another, *Baro* singers arise to call out the rhythmical poetry honouring Sheikh Hussein and to receive the response of the congregation who take up the singer's last word as a chorus.

Hermits, wandering mystics whose hair hangs down in butter-smeared ringlets, even some small children, these people of the *Baro* – like the people within the tomb – are occupied by a force beyond themselves. They say that they are not responsible for the words that come to them, that they are merely channels of communication between the parallel universes of the sacred and the profane. "If I should lose the gift," one later explains, "it would be terrible – as though I were a beehive without bees . . ."

CAVERNS MEASURELESS TO MAN

The pilgrimage used to take place once a year in the month of February to mark the anniversary of Sheikh Hussein's death, but now a second pilgrimage, loosely linked with *Mauwlid* (a pan-Islamic festival that marks the birth of the Prophet Mohammed), occurs later in the year.

The rituals last for approximately two weeks. When they are over the vast crowds of people who have gathered – rarely less than fifty thousand – disperse across the countryside. Some, for whom this has been a once-in-a-lifetime experience, return to their homes. Others, however – those who know no other existence than the open road – make their way south through the Bale foothills to another shrine devoted to another Muslim saint.

At some time in the distant past, just as Sheikh Hussein had followed the course of the Shebelle, a man called Sof Omar followed the Juba River from the Somali coast deep into the hinterland. Towards the end of his journey he abandoned the main stream and walked along the banks of a tributary known as the Weyb – and here, eventually, in a low valley lost among dense thorn groves, he stumbled across the entrance of the massive cave-system that was to become his home, and from which he was to perform his miracles.

A savage place, holy and enchanted, this subterranean kingdom was hallowed ground long before Sof Omar first explored its chambers of moss-covered stone. Neither has Allah's name banished the familiars of the older gods: on the contrary, turbulent and malign *ayanas* seem to swirl everywhere above the dark and deep-flowing river.

Carved out over countless aeons by the perennial flood and recess of the Weyb itself, the Sof Omar cave system surpasses even the opium-inspired fantasies of Samuel Taylor Coleridge. Here, the ghostly music that the poet heard is replaced by the soft moan and exhalation of currents of air as they move through high, eroded oriels and among lofty pillars and flying buttresses of stone. Now and then, also, pouring out from hidden declivities, echoing between barely visible walls, the waters of the Weyb churn and boil as though agitated by the passage of something huge and violent . . .

Part Muslim, part infidel, the members of an arcane priestood attend to the mysteries of the Sof Omar caves. Robed in rags, these secretive men roam the galleries offering up prayers and decorating the fetish trees with strips of coloured cloth. The pilgrims also leave votive offerings: a gutted and beheaded goat at the foot of a stalagmite, tokens of leather and beads dangling from ledges above the river and other even stranger gifts.

It is surely a profound irony that the saint who came here to convert the heathen to Islam so many centuries ago has himself been transformed by the invincible power of superstition into a pagan spirit whose presence is both exalted and menacing.

OVERLEAF: Pilgrims come on foot, on horseback and by mule from distances of up to 600 miles to pay homage to Sheikh Hussein, the thirteenth-century mystic prophet who lies buried in the town of the same name. This pilgrimage takes place twice a year, once in February–March to celebrate the anniversary of the death of Sheikh Hussein and once in August–September to celebrate the birth of the Prophet Mohammed. On each occasion, approximately fifty thousand people come from all parts of the Horn and stay for about two weeks.

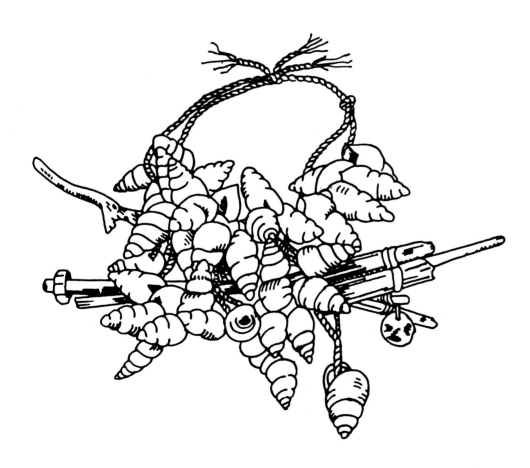

Gariba gypsies often wear elaborate necklaces made of shells or beads which serve as talismans offering protection during their long pilgrimage to the holy site of Sheikh Hussein.

The tomb of Sheikh Hussein is covered with colourful cloths to mark the
occasion of a celebration. Pligrims enter the tomb daily to benefit from the
healing powers of this ancient miracle worker.

LEFT, ABOVE AND OVERLEAF: Pilgrims sit for hours inside the tomb of Sheikh Hussein. They caress and kiss the smooth stone walls which have been touched in this manner for hundreds of years. Chalk stones from the floor are crushed into powder and then mixed with saliva; the resulting paste is smeared over their bodies as a cure for all kinds of ailments. Some pilgrims push themselves through a small opening to an inner sanctum where the saint's body lies.

The ancient mosque built by Sheikh Hussein himself is the second most holy place here. Sheikhs, Imams and Hajis sit in the inner sanctum of the mosque reading out loud passages from the Koran. The pages of their books are illuminated by narrow shafts of light passing through openings in the ceiling of the mosque.

Groups of gypsies, known as *Gariba*, make their base at the site of two entwined fig trees, said to be the place where Sheikh Hussein prayed and taught children. The *Gariba* come largely from animist cultures and are now practising a crude form of Islam. They are looked down upon by orthodox Muslims because not all their beliefs are in accord with the Koran and because their appearance is wild and unkempt.

LEFT: The gypsies sleep within the walls of the compound encircling the tomb of Sheikh Hussein. Each carries a forked staff in a tradition that dates back to pagan times.

ABOVE: A young gypsy boy, a gifted *Baro* singer, chants phrases in honour of Sheikh Hussein.

OVERLEAF: Each afternoon, crowds gather outside the gates of the tomb for *Baro* singing – a form of antiphonal chanting in which rhyming poetry honouring Sheikh Hussein is sung. The *Baro* leader calls out a verse, then points his staff at the audience who take up the last word as a chorus.

LEFT: When the *Baro* leader chants, he cups his ear to keep out distracting noise and thus to hold the tone. Alongside the *Baro* singing, *Dibba* dancing (ABOVE) melds the animistic heritage with Islamic traditions. The wild emotive movements of the dancers, accompanied by drums and clapping, are a form of exorcism of evil *zar* spirits. As the dance becomes more frenetic, women possessed by spirits swoon in trance states exorcizing the demons within.

LEFT: Holy men chant with upraised arms, punctuating the wild rhythms of the *Baro*.

ABOVE: Three sheikhs gaze in wonderment. The one on the left is chewing *chat*, a leafy narcotic stimulant which leaves a green residue on the lips, inhibits the appetite and heightens awareness.

OVERLEAF: When pilgrims leave the site of Sheikh Hussein, they often visit the sacred caves of Sof Omar, a sixteenth-century Islamic mystic. Through the vast limestone caverns flows the river Weyb. Within the cave system are small mosques where pilgrims pay homage to Sof Omar. To ensure that their prayers are answered, they tear off strips of clothing and leave them behind to keep the saint mindful of their visit.

CHAPTER SEVEN

PEOPLES OF THE MORNING

Southwest Ethiopia: the Konso, Borana and Hamar

s far to the west of the Juba River as Lake Stephanie, the badlands of southern Ethiopia and of northern Kenya form a single harsh ecosystem that has been mastered by a single resiliant tribe, the Borana, who are regarded with a special kind of awe by other members of the great and scattered Oromo family to which they belong. As one elder explains:

"The Borana are the first born. They are the people of the morning. They are nearer to *Waq*. Our people have a feeling that *Waq* gives all good things to the Borana and through them to us."[1]

Such notions are rooted in the widespread belief that the Borana are of the purest, finest and oldest stock. More importantly, it is felt that this tribe alone has upheld Oromo honour by refusing to abandon the ancestral way of life believed to have been enjoyed in an idealized past: "when all our people inhabited a land of marvels and when the white cattle yielded so much milk and meat that men neither ploughed nor sowed."[2]

Although resonant of myth and fable, the folk wisdom contains many ethnographical truths. The Borana *are* descended from the very first Oromo groups to have established themselves in southern Ethiopia during the diaspora of the fifteenth and sixteenth centuries. They have never since vacated the lands that they then seized. And they remain uncompromising pastoralists who depend almost exclusively upon their livestock for subsistence at a time when other Oromos have become traders, city dwellers, villagers, or farmers.

Unlike the Somalis, their ancient enemies to the east, the Borana make little use of goats and camels. Instead their lives revolve around cattle – which they love and revere. Their herds consist predominantly of a breed of shorthorn East African humped Zebu known colloquially as the Boran Zebu. Though hardy, capable of tolerating great heat, and highly resistant to indigenous stock diseases, these animals cannot endure the rigours of a desert environment unless

LEFT: The Konso commemorate dead heroes with carved wooden figures known as *waga* (which means, literally, "something of the grandfathers").

Above: Cast iron or aluminium phallic ornaments, called *kallaacha*, worn on the forehead by Konso elders during certain passages of the *Gada* ceremony.
Below: Wire combs used for scratching the scalp underneath the clay hair buns worn by men of the Omo River region.

they are watered frequently. In addition they cannot be walked great distances between pastures.

Borana society is thus characterized by semi-nomadic pastoralism based upon seasonal settlements. Typically, these "villages" will uproot and move several times a year; nevertheless, they tend to acquire an aura of permanence enhanced by proper wattle-and-daub houses.

Villages are not the only relatively "fixed" institutions of Borana life. A considerable industry – in which a number of clans participate – involves the mining of sodium deposits from the floors of several of the extinct volcanic caldera found in this region. The salt thus produced is an important ecological resource that meets both human and livestock needs. Of greater importance still, however, are the Boranas' desert wells.

Recent geological surveys indicate that there are no more than thirty-five productive aquifers in this area – all of which, without benefit of science, have long ago been discovered and thoroughly exploited. Indeed, at each location there are often as many as twenty functioning wells. Some are sunk deep through the surface rock. Others take the form of wide, shallow shafts dug out of alluvial soils like sand or gravel.

Wells of this latter type are still occasionally opened up; however, no new deep wells have been made within living memory and the technology employed in their excavation has been forgotten. Descending thirty metres or more, the deepest shafts look like particularly formidable undertakings and could only have been sunk by an organized society capable of mobilising substantial resources.

The Borana today are not wealthy – as the construction of their wells suggests they must once have been in the past. They do, however, remain highly organized, disciplined and cooperative. They have strong ritual sanctions against fighting and killing within the tribe. Indeed, it is believed that *Waq*, the sky god, would withold the rains if one Borana should ever spill the blood of another.

This emphasis on peace and harmony within Borana society, however, is completely reversed with regard to outsiders. The Borana are capable of extreme violence when protecting their pastures and hard-earned water rights against the encroachments of other tribes. Neither is this aspect of their nature confined to legitimate self-defence: on the contrary, an aggressive and warlike front is maintained towards almost all non-Borana (with the exception of a very few allied groups), and virtually any stranger is regarded as fair game for ambush and murder.

For these people, as for the Afar (to whom they are distantly related), homicide is much more than just a means of getting enemies neatly and permanently out of the way; it also has social and ritual significance of a high order.

Thus, although there have been profound cultural changes as a result of the increasing imposition of Ethiopian and Kenyan law, reinforced by police posts and occasional army patrols, the honour of each and every Borana male of warrior age continues to be bound up with the killing of other men. If a homicide takes place in the absence of independent witnesses capable of verifying it, then the penis and testicles of the victim are normally hacked off and carried back to the village as proof positive that murder has been done. By demonstrating his machismo and bravery in this manner a successful fighter can earn from his comrades the much-coveted epithet *diira* – meaning "virile". He will also be able to take pride in nicknames like *jaba* (tough) or *korma* (a bull).

The premium put on casual brutality is such that a Borana who has failed to participate in a raid – or, at the very least, to murder a hapless passer-by – is not likely to be welcomed as a husband by any potential bride or to be seen as a suitable son-in-law by her family. By contrast, an acknowledged killer is given gifts of stock, lavished with sexual favours, and allowed to wear special earrings, necklaces and ivory armlets. More important to the murderer than all these badges of rank, however, is the fact he earns the right to "make his head" – to grow a male hair tuft which will instantly transform him into the darling of every eligible girl.[3]

There can be no doubt that this top knot is symbolically associated with an erect penis. The practice seems odd until we remember that Oromo warriors in the sixteenth and seventeenth centuries frequently adorned themselves with the genitals of the enemies they had killed – in some cases wearing them on their foreheads until they had completely decayed and dropped off.[4]

This same explanation perhaps also accounts for the styling of the Boranas' most prized items of ritual paraphernalia – the phallus-shaped *kallaacha* which are cast from iron or aluminium and attached to men's heads during the *gada* ceremonies that mark the transitions from one age-grade to the next.[5] Since these proud nomads refuse to stoop to manual trades like metalwork they are obliged to rely on the skilled smiths of an allied tribe to manufacture the *kallaacha* for them.

Known as the Konso, that tribe plays Dr Jekyll to the Boranas' Mr Hyde.

PEOPLE OF WOOD AND STONE

Hard working, materialistic, sedentary cultivators, the Konso do their best (though not always successfully) to remain at peace with all their neighbours. The Borana on the other hand, as we have seen, are: "a nation at once pastoral and warlike who live without any settled habitation, whose only wealth is their flocks and herds, and yet who have carried on, through all the ages, an hereditary war with all mankind . . ."[6]

Nevertheless, the two tribes share many of the same cultural traits.

Both, for example, worship the sky god *Waq*, both venerate serpents and both display elements of an ancestor cult. This latter characteristic is particularly well developed among the Konso who commemorate dead heroes with carved wooden figures known as *waga*, "something of the grandfathers". Presenting to public view the sum total of a man's achievements, these stark and eerie totems huddle in the midst of open fields or by roadsides, and depict not only the deceased but also his wives, the enemies he has slain in battle and any "noble" animals – such as a lion or a leopard – that he may have killed during the course of his life.[7]

Close cousins, whose family trees in fact coincide some four hundred years in the past, the Konso and the Boran today speak Hamitic languages that are virtually indistinguishable from one another. Both have very similar age set institutions. Both also hold elaborate initiation ceremonies to mark the rites of passage from one grade to the next, and both make use of identical phallic *kallaacha* during these ceremonies.[8]

It is here, however, that the resemblances stop and the differences begin. Nevertheless, even in these differences a special kind of link remains.

At all levels the two peoples exist in a state of symbiosis. It is, for example, not just *kallaacha* that the proud and disdainful pastoralists buy from their settled, assiduous kin. The Konso are also skilled in weaving, pottery and other crafts and are thus able to supply the Borana with the colourful cotton cloths that they much admire, with blankets and also with a range of utensils that would otherwise not be easily available to them. More importantly, Konsoland represents an emporium of agricultural produce while Borana country is a vast meat market: a lively two-way trade thus goes on throughout the year, in which the nomads exchange their livestock for the farmers' plentiful crops.

It is as cultivators, certainly, that the Konso excel. Their territory, on the eastern rim of the Lower Omo valley, lies in mountainous terrain some thirty miles south of Lake Chamo at an altitude of approximately 5,000 feet. Despite plentiful rainfall, this is not promising country for agriculture for the simple reason that the many steep inclines make erosion caused by rapid water run-off an ever-present threat. The Konso have accepted this state of affairs and have made the best of what nature has given them by creating elaborate terracing buttressed with stone. Extensive and intricate, this system preserves the fertility of the friable topsoils and prevents them from being washed down into the valleys below.

The net effect – achieved by months of painstaking, backbreaking labour – is a

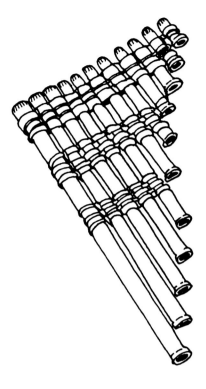

Above: Reed "panpipes" played by Konso men.
Below: Decorated calabashes (incised and rubbed with charcoal) used for carrying milk, animal fat and grains.

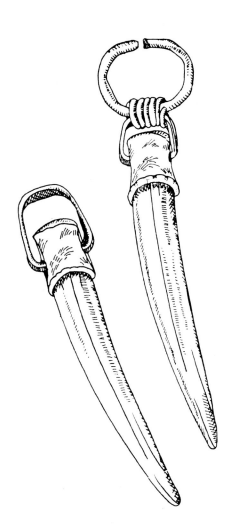

Top left and facing page: Carved wooden headrests used by men of the Omo River region to protect their hairstyles while sleeping.
Above: Tusk pendants worn by Mursi and Bodi men as signs of bravery and status.

rather beautiful one. Furthermore, the stone shoring employed in the terraces is echoed by the dry stone walls that surround Konso villages and that protect the lower-lying fields from flash floods and marauding cattle. Stone, used also for grinding grain, sharpening knives and spears, making anvils, lining wells, and constructing dams, is as one anthropologist has commented: "as much a part of Konso life as soil. Their use of stone gives clarity and definition to their homesteads . . . it [also] conveys a sense of harmony, order and industry and is, in these respects, a true expression of their values."[9]

Konso industriousness finds its vehicle in a cooperative ethic that enables each farmer to enlist the support of communal work parties from his own and surrounding villages to build terraces and walls and to sow and harvest the principal crops – at least twenty-four different varieties of millet are grown as well as wheat and barley, maize, peas, beans, potatoes, marrows, bananas, cotton and coffee. Great emphasis is placed on productivity. Indeed, so conscientious are these people that whole villages have been known to turn out into the fields at midnight during rainstorms to ensure that the water is flowing well and not running to waste.[10]

Not all aspects of life, however, are so dominated by hard work. The Konso love music and make use of a wide range of instruments for religious and ceremonial purposes and for entertainment. Young children amuse themselves with bullroarers, while many women and boys are expert flute players. The *krar*, which is related to the lyre and is found in different forms in all parts of Ethiopia, is popular with males, as is the five-stringed *dita* (which somewhat resembles a guitar). Konso men also form themselves into teams in order to produce concertos on specially evolved "panpipes" – each member of the village orchestra is responsible for playing and sustaining just a single note.

HEART AND EYES

The Konsos' green and densely farmed mountains topped by orderly villages and neat, round houses, form an outpost of sedate, evolved culture in the midst of a strange, wild country that grows ever more primal and savage as one journeys towards the Ethio-Sudanese border. Certainly, beyond the terraced and productive highlands, there is no "civilization" at all in the Western sense, and almost no "development" (unless, within that much-abused term, one counts the lamentable introduction of automatic rifles to peoples who are otherwise virtually living in the Stone Age).

As though to underscore the social transition that is about to take place, the land slopes sharply downhill to the west of the last Konso habitations and even the flora and fauna begin to change. Without any particular line of demarcation, orderly fields simply give way to savannahs interspersed with patches of dense bush.

Here, in this difficult country, live a people known as the Hamar who seem to straddle a cultural divide between the Hamitic races of the Horn (like the Borana and the Konso) and other more distant groups (classified by ethnologists as "Nilotic" because they live in the environs of the great Nile river).

The Hamar are a seminomadic tribe with a total population of about fifteen thousand and, like the Borana, they are pastoralists. Although they are known for their skills in pottery, beekeeping and smithying, their herds – especially their cattle – are the focus of their culture and of their socioeconomic life. Even their vocabulary reflects this concern: there are at least twenty-seven words for the subtle variations of colour and texture of cattle – and every Hamar man has several names, including a goat name and a cow name.

These are a superstitious people who believe that evil and bad luck (*mingi*) exist in certain unholy or impure things. Twins, a child born out of wedlock, and children whose upper milk teeth come before their lower ones, are considered to possess *mingi* and, for this reason, they are thrown into the forest to die. Hamar parents would rather lose a child than risk crop failure, drought, or ill health in the family.

Both men and women set great store by their appearance, and decorate themselves beautifully. Their bodies are well oiled and ornamented with colourful beads. Their hair-styles vary. To indicate that they have killed an enemy, men sport clay hair buns into which ostrich feathers are inserted. Women tend to wear their hair in short tufts rolled in ochre and fat or in long twisted strands. A man flirts in dancing by cocking his head of feathers at a woman; her response is to flick her long, heavy strands of hair at him.

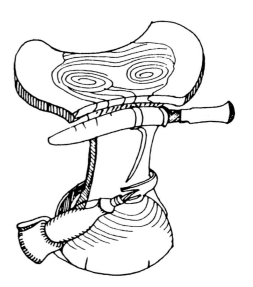

Like the Borana, the Hamar have evolved an elaborate age-grading system charac-terized by periodic "rites of passage" which celebrate transitions from one age grade to the next. Hairstyles are important here, too, in marking these stages.

By far the most significant ceremony is known as the "jumping of the bull". For the novices – passing from boyhood into early adulthood – this dramatic ritual represents a life-changing event. Several weeks before the ceremony is due, the boy to be initiated delivers invitations to his neighbours in the form of a blade of dried grass knotted in several places. These knots are a calendar of days and each day the guest must untie one of the knots until the day of the ceremony arrives. The novice also carries with him a carved wooden phallus known as the *bokko* which he hands to girls he meets along the way; they must kiss it three times as a form of blessing and then return it to him.

Each novice undergoes an individual ceremony, an event which usually lasts three days. On the first day several hundred guests gather, among them the *maz* (recently initiated men) who arrive in a long line and participate in a coffee-drinking ceremony.

Aged between twenty and twenty-five, the *maz* belong to a special category in Hamar society. Since they have already jumped the bull themselves they are considered to have left their youth behind; at the same time, however, they are still too young to marry and thus are not yet thought of as properly "grown up". Their principal respon-sibility is to support the novice throughout the rituals of preparation preceding the jumping, but they are also required to participate with him in various ways in the initia-tion ceremony itself.

An early task, for which only the *maz* are ritually qualified, involves whipping the novice's young female relatives. Far from being reluctant to suffer the considerable pain involved, the girls beg to be chastised – since in this way they can demonstrate the strength of their devotion to the boy.

On the day of the initiation itself, the *maz* are charged with the important job of steadying the cattle over which the novice must jump. Late in the afternoon they line up some thirty beasts side by side and hold them closely together in a specially designated area which has a clearly marked symbolic entrance at one end and an equally clearly marked exit at the other. The novice is then brought in, totally naked (as he was at the moment of birth), his arms pinioned by two of the *maz*. When they release him, he charges at breakneck speed towards the cattle, vaults onto the back of the first and then runs across all the remaining animals. At the far end of the line he jumps down, turns around, then leaps back up again and repeats the performance in the other direction. Altogether he makes four runs and finally – if everything has gone well – the *maz* lead him out through the exit amid wild dancing and exultation.

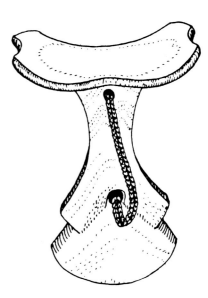

For a novice to fall during the jumping is considered bad luck – and for this reason, great efforts are made by the *maz* to keep the cattle still. A single fall incurs no penalty and is blamed on the movement of the animals. Any boy who fails to complete his four runs, however, will be publicly humiliated: he will be whipped by his female relatives in the middle of the initiation ground and thereafter, for the rest of his life, he will be teased, insulted and beaten by both men and women. Understandably, few novices allow themselves to fail in this way.

After he has satisfactorily "jumped the bull", a boy is considered to have put aside childish things and is allowed to join the *maz* – thus taking a vital step forward on the road to full adult status. In this intensely conservative society, true manhood is thought to come slowly. Indeed, the Hamar say that maturity is only reached when the heart moves into the eyes – that is, when the eyes see with the heart.

ABOVE: For the Konso, wood and stone are the two most highly valued building materials.

RIGHT: A woman climbs out of the elaborate wooden entrance to her family compound. Wood is also used for building huts, meeting houses and the fences which line the passageways throughout the village.

PRECEDING PAGES (210 AND 211): In the rocky terrain of southwest Ethiopia, Konso farmers, threatened by the continuous erosion of their fields, have perfected the art of terracing to maintain the fertility of the soil. Corn, sorghum, beans and cotton are grown in rotation throughout the year.

OVERLEAF: In a Konso village several huts are grouped together in one compound. Earthen pots are placed in the smoke hole of each hut to protect the interior from rain. Within the compound a woman prepares millet and sorghum to feed her family.

In addition to working in the fields, a Konso woman's everyday activities
include carrying fire-wood, grinding corn and caring for her children.

When a hero or important man has died, *waga* figures (RIGHT) are carved in his honour. They are placed in and around the fields, and not necessarily where the man has been buried. The deceased is usually represented in the centre of the *waga* group and flanked by his wives. On the outside stand any enemies he may have killed, carved in an abstract and phallic fashion. Fierce animals he has slain, such as a leopard, a lion or a crocodile, will also be depicted and placed at his feet. In front of the central figure, representing the deceased, is his shield. On his forehead a phallic symbol is carved. This is similar to the *kallaacha* (ABOVE), made of iron or aluminium and worn on the foreheads of elders during ceremonies.

OVERLEAF: The *waga* figure on the left represents a Borana man. The small point carved on the top of his head represents the Borana hair tuft. The *waga* figure on the right represents a dead hero with a *kallaacha* on his forehead.

218

In southern Ethiopia, Chew Bet, the crater lake of an extinct volcano, is an important source of salt for the pastoral Borana. Men armed with poles dig up large clods of salt-bearing mud from the bed of the Chew Bet crater lake. The mud is then either put to dry in mounds at the water's edge or packed by women so that it can be transported by mule to the village.

The black mud is dug up during the rainy season and the salt extracted from it is given to cattle to build up animal strength. During the dry season the Borana dig deep beneath the exposed surface to collect the white salt, which is used for human consumption – the deeper they dig the better the quality of the salt.

OVERLEAF: In a typical village of the seminomadic Borana in southern Ethiopia, termite mounds are prominent features among the portable huts.

Traditional Borana wells are sunk through the surface rock to a depth of 100 feet or more. A single well provides level terraces where herdsmen stand passing buckets of water from the bottom to the top, chanting rhythmically as they work. Many hours of work are required to fill the animal trough at the top of the well.

OVERLEAF: A Hamar child carries his goat to a shallow well in a sandy river bed. After the animals have been watered, children linger on to play.

229

Hamar men and women pay great attention to the styling and decoration of hair. Hair styling enhances beauty and signifies status, bravery and courage.

Clay hair buns are worn by Hamar men who have killed either an enemy or a dangerous animal such as a lion or a leopard. Symbolizing courage, the clay bun is usually remade every three to six months and can be worn for a period of up to one year after the kill. A small holder, made of macrame, is put into the front bun to display ostrich feathers for special occasions. The clay is plastered directly on to the head. The front part of the bun is covered in white chalk and then splattered with ochre paint. The back bun is left a natural grey colour.

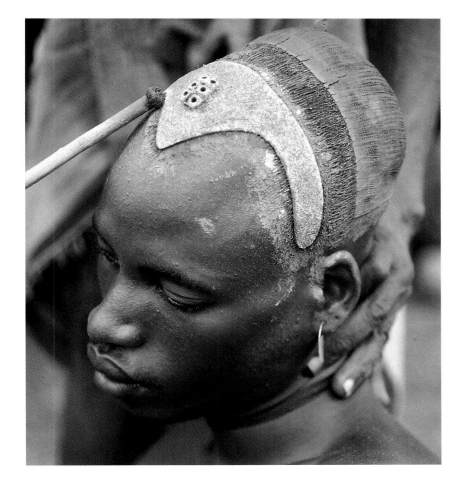

At the "jumping of the bull" ceremony, which marks the initiation of young men into adulthood, girls with trumpets herald the arrival of the *maz* – those Hamar males who have already undergone this rite of passage.

ABOVE: At the "jumping of the bull" ceremony, the *maz* (recently initiated young men) take part in a ritual coffee-drinking ceremony, which is regarded as a blessing.
RIGHT: Young women, related to the novice who is about to be initiated, beg to be whipped by the *maz*: this ordeal reveals their ability to endure pain on behalf of the boy they love; the more numerous and extensive the scars, the deeper the girls' devotion to the boy who is about to become a man.

SUCCEEDING PAGES (240 AND 241): Preparations begin for the "jumping of the bull" ceremony. As the animals (between fifteen and thirty) are herded together, the most recently initiated boy, smeared with oil and charcoal, circles them.

(242 AND 243): The intiate takes a running leap onto the back of the first bull and then charges across the backs of all the others. He must repeat this four times in order to prove his manhood. If he falls off, he will be whipped and teased mercilessly by the women.

ABOVE AND RIGHT: On the day after the "jumping of the bull" ceremony, women gather together, beautifully attired in their beaded skins and iron jewellery. Their hair is rubbed with fat into small balls and covered with ochre. This hairstyle is frequently set off with aluminium plaques in the shape of ducks' bills which project dramatically from the forehead. Courtship dances follow and continue for the following two days and nights.

OVERLEAF: Married women favour a hairstyle of long, twisted strands rubbed in ochre. Around their necks they wear *esente* (torques made of iron wrapped in leather). These engagement presents, indicative of their future husband's wealth, are made by the village smith and worn for life. An upper torque, the *bignere*, may only be worn by a man's first wife. Added at the time of marriage, its distinctive iron protrusion is both a phallic and a status symbol.

CHAPTER EIGHT

PEOPLES OF THE WILDERNESS

*The Omo River and Southwest Ethiopia:
the Bumi, Mursi, Anuak, Nuer and Surma*

 ew areas remain in Africa that can be described as true wilderness. But the country of the Hamar would seem fully to qualify for that definition. It is a lost world enclosed by Abyssinian mountains 13,000 feet high, by the Sudan's impenetrable Nile swamps, and by the desolate barrens of the Ethio-Kenya borderlands.

Forgotten by history, and as yet inadequately charted by geographers, the Lower Omo Valley forms the approximate centre of this remote zone. Here, side by side with the Hamar, a number of small bands of pastoralists and subsistence farmers – the Karo, for example – coexist with groups of hunter-gatherers in a state of wild, almost primordial innocence. Like the Hamar, these peoples show many cultural traits that are common to all members of the great Hamitic family; but they also have other, less familiar characteristics that betray their connections with peoples whose homes lie far beyond the margins of the Horn.

North and west of the Omo as far as the Baro river we begin to encounter other groups, such as the Bumi, the Anuak and the Nuer, who are more properly defined as sons of the Nile than sons of Noah – for they all speak Nilotic languages of the southern Sudanese type. Scattered among these peoples, furthermore, there are small communities speaking languages that appear to be completely dislocated from those of any of their neighbours. Described by some authorities as Nilotes, by others as Nilo-Hamites, it has also been suggested that these clans – which include the Mursi,

the Bodi and the Surma – are in fact the remnants of a very ancient layer of Hamitic peoples pushed west and north across the Omo river by successive waves of invasion from the east.[1]

All efforts to fit the various tribes of this region into neat ethnic and linguistic categories are doomed to failure and anyway shed no light on the realities of their daily lives. Stated simply, one cannot assume that relatives are also friends. The Mursi, for example, are often at war with their kin and neighbours the Bodi, and permanently at war with the Hamar – from whom they are separated by a large tract of uninhabited bush. Sometimes the Mursi and the Bodi make peace in order to fight the Hamar together, sometimes they fight

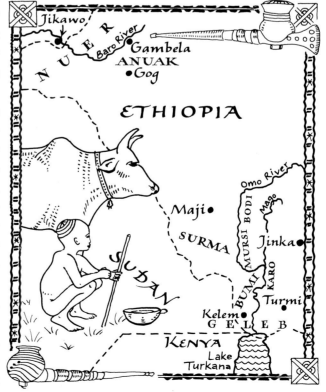

LEFT: Surma woman of southwest Ethiopia, with characteristic clay lip plate.

249

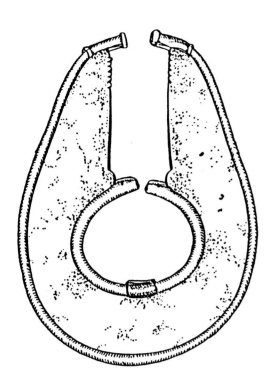

them separately and sometimes the Bodi do not fight them at all.[2] The Hamar, for their part, are frequently at war with their cousins the Karo. Meanwhile the Bumi fight both the Hamar *and* the Karo and also hit the Surma whenever they can.[3]

The net effect, particularly on the choicest lands close to the Omo River, is of a war of all against all in which life can be every bit as nasty, brutish and short as the philosopher Hobbes imagined. It is thus not surprising that a great many of the inhabitants of this region display the stumps of severed limbs and the blemishes of old wounds. They do so with pride, for such injuries bear witness to the dastardly attacks that they have survived and the splendid raids in which they have participated.

It is other more important badges of valour, however, that are most commonly and most blatantly touted: these take the form of self-inflicted scars, patterned according to a secret code and imbued with honour.

Typical in this respect are the deep horseshoe-shaped incisions that Mursi and Bodi warriors make on their upper arms whenever they succeed in murdering a member of another group. In theory the cuts are made on the right arm for a male victim and on the left arm for a female victim; in practice homicide is so frequent that the more successful fighters quickly run out of room on their arms and thereafter must resort to their thighs and eventually other parts of the body as well.

Above: Iron wrist knife with its leather guard which can be removed to reveal a razor sharp blade for fighting.
Below: Iron finger knives worn by men of the Omo river region.

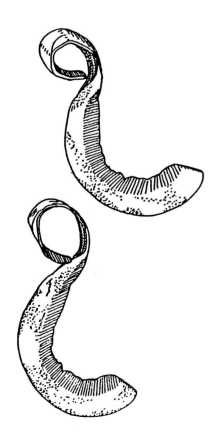

RITUAL DUELLING

The extensive scarification of young men attests to the existence of a high degree of hostility throughout the Lower Omo valley. Nevertheless, relationships *within* each of the groups living in this area tend to be calm, cooperative and peaceful – thanks, in part, to orderly (if complicated) age-grading systems. The unruly energies that might lead to fighting between age mates do, of course, exist; rather than being allowed to disrupt tribal harmony, however, they are typically channelled into ritualized duelling in which killing is explicitly forbidden.

Among both the Surma and the Mursi a single-combat sport of physical skill, known as *donga* (stick fighting), has evolved into something of an art form that allows young men to take part in competitions of strength and masculinity, earn honour among their peers and win the hands of girls in marriage without serious risk of death.

Surrounded by cheering spectators, the duelists – swathed in protective clothing – measure up to each other in specially prepared clearings. Each contestant is armed with a hardwood pole, carved into a phallus shape at the tip, about six feet in length and weighing just under two pounds. In the attacking position, this pole is gripped at its base with both hands, the left above the right, to give maximum swing and leverage.

Each player lands as many blows as possible upon his adversary, the object of the exercise being to knock him down and completely eliminate him from the game. Severe injuries are often inflicted, but the referee usually intervenes before a fatal blow is delivered. If a fighter kills his opponent, he and his family are banished from the village, his property is confiscated and if he or his family have a daughter she may be given to the victim's relatives as compensation.

Selected from the two warrior age grades, players are generally unmarried men between sixteen and thirty-two years old and represent local "teams". Often as many as fifty people will compete, and all of them get the chance to fight at least once. At the end of every bout, however, the loser must accept his defeat gracefully and withdraw – while the winner goes on to face another winner. In this way the field eventually narrows down to just two surviving contestants, one of whom will emerge not only as the victor of this last bout but also of the contest as a whole. The winner is borne away on a platform of poles to a group of girls waiting at the side of the arena who decide among themselves which of them will ask for his hand in marriage.

Amongst the Mursi and the Surma, taking part in the *donga* stick fight is considered to be more important than winning it. Thus, even if he was knocked out early in the contest, a brave and determined duellist will still be heaped with honour. He will marry in the usual way – that is by chosing his own wife to be and offering her father the required bride price for her hand.

THE ART OF INNOCENCE

The wilderness peoples of the Lower Omo lack any form of advanced material culture but nevertheless inhabit a rich symbolic universe. Symbolism is everything – scars, ostrich feathers, topknots, jewellery and even certain items of clothing all convey significant and unambiguous messages, as we have already seen.

The Surma and the Mursi are part of that small remaining group of peoples anywhere in the world whose women still wear lip plates – and, once again, these have a function that is almost purely symbolic. There are several theories as to why the use of lip plates was first adopted: perhaps to discourage slavers looking for unblemished girls; or perhaps to prevent evil from entering the body by way of the mouth (since these people believe that evil penetrates the body through its orifices); or to indicate the number of cattle required by the wearer's family for her hand in marriage.

Today it is the third of these theories that is the one seen in practical use. In her early twenties a woman's lower lip will be pierced and then progressively stretched over the period of a year – the size of the lip plate determining the size of the bride price. A large lip plate will bring fifty head of cattle. A heavy iron puberty apron and many armlets will likewise help to increase the young woman's appeal.

It would be wrong to suggest that all forms of decoration are symbolic, however. Purely aesthetic considerations, too, are to be seen at work in the Lower Omo – notably among the Surma and the Karo (see Chapter Nine) who have developed elaborate and idiosyncratic traditions of body painting. Before every ceremony, Surma men and women decorate their bodies to make themselves more appealing to the opposite sex. Men also paint their bodies to increase their power in stick fighting and to intimidate their enemies when they go cattle raiding.

The best artists are generally male – and they paint not just each other but also the women and children of the tribe. Using local chalk mixed with water, they create many and varied patterns including swirls, stripes, flower and star designs – all of which are enjoyed solely for their beauty. This activity is one of the main forms of artistic expression available to the Surma and the Karo. Creatively at work, the painter reveals himself as an artist, and the human form – viewed as a living sculpture and as a vehicle for the imagination – becomes itself a work of art.

The innocent enthusiasm that body painting generates, the inspiration that it expresses, and the close social bonds that it reaffirms, all suggest that the Lower Omo is a place of joy and hope as well as of intertribal competition and war, a place in which mankind is still capable of appreciating simple pleasures, still filled with laughter, and still unashamedly amazed at the wonders that the world has to offer.

SUCCEEDING PAGES (252 AND 253): The Bumi live in a remote wilderness area along the banks of the Omo river. Traditionally hunters and gatherers, they hunt crocodiles in the waters of the Omo and subsidize their diet by growing millet and corn.

(254 AND 255): A Bumi elder inspects the granaries on the edge of his village.

(256 AND 257): In the family compound of an Anuak village, women grind and sift maize, which they make into a porridge, the staple food of their diet.

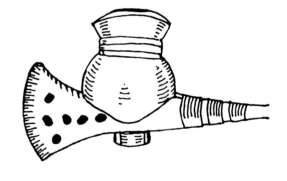

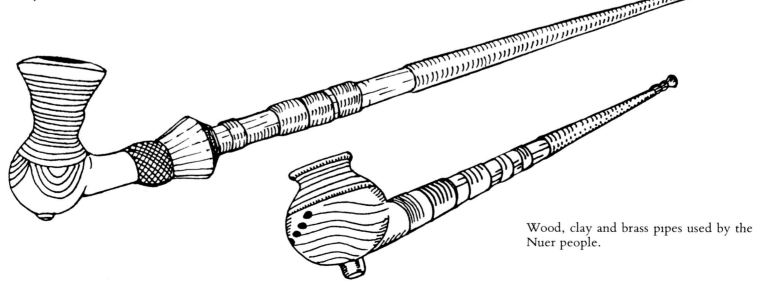

Wood, clay and brass pipes used by the Nuer people.

251

In contrast to the pastoralists of the Lower Omo valley, the Anuak boast well-organized agriculture in addition to their cattle. An Anuak woman (RIGHT) pounds maize with a heavy wooden pole. The Nuer to the northwest are pure pastoralists who are noted for the strength of their bond to their cattle. A Nuer man (ABOVE) smokes a traditional pipe of locally grown tobacco. His pipe is made of clay, brass and bamboo. The parallel lines of scarification running across his forehead identify him as a Nuer.

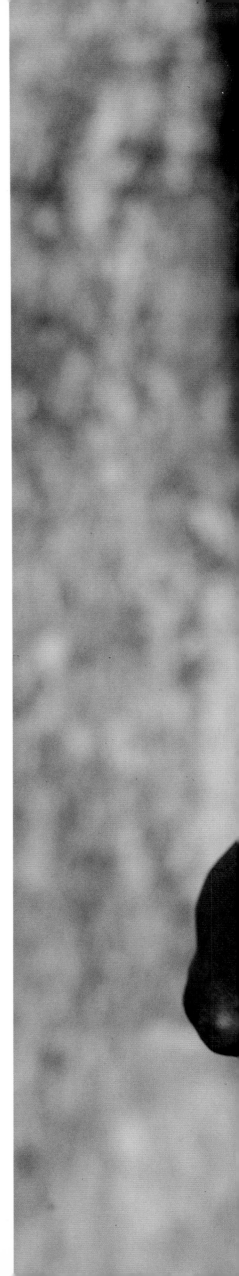

Bumi men decorate their faces with scarified designs to establish tribal identity and to enhance their physical appearance. Like the Hamar, they wear elaborate clay hair buns, symbolic of bravery and courage.

The Mursi, living to the north of the Bumi on the Omo river, specialize in the scarification of the body as well as the face. Men (ABOVE) and women (RIGHT) see body scarification as a means of attracting the opposite sex.

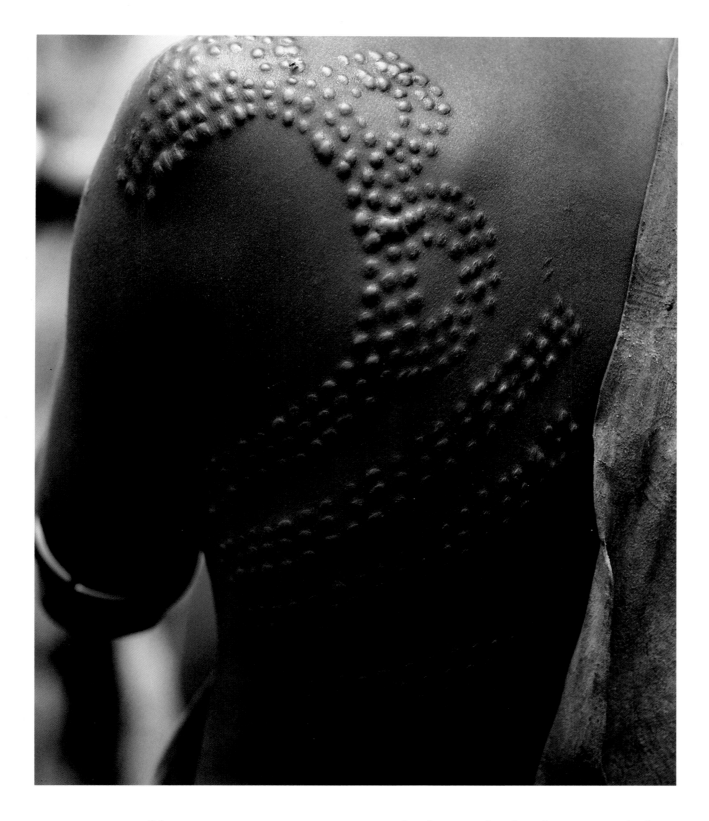

OVERLEAF: West of the Omo river, in a mountainous region bordering Sudan, live the Surma – who have been forced out of their ancestral homelands by the Bumi, their traditional enemies. Guns have replaced spears in order to protect their families and discourage cattle raiding.

Surma children often paint themselves as identical twins. The snake dance is one of their favourite games. Squatting on the ground, the children form a long line and hop slowly forward like grasshoppers singing in unison the words: "Our mother, our apple, our fruit."

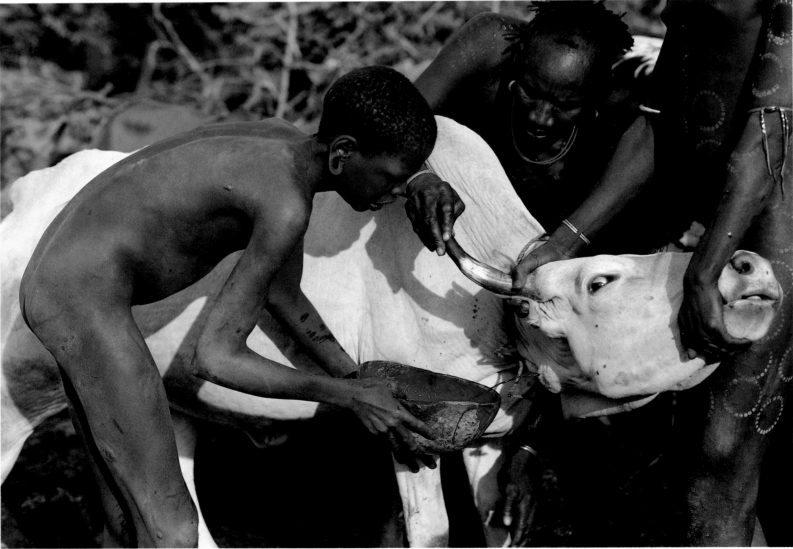

268   The Surma live primarily on a diet of milk and blood, seasonally supplemented by maize and millet. An arrow is shot a quarter of an inch into the jugular vein of a young heifer to obtain just enough blood to fill a calabash. The animal is never killed; instead the wound is sutured with a compress of wet mud. Young boys drink blood to grow, and men to gain strength.

Between the ages of twenty and twenty-five, a lip plate is inserted into a woman's lower lip. The process begins six months prior to marriage with the piercing of the lower lip. Successive stretching is achieved by placing increasingly larger plates into the pierced lip. The final size of the plate is an indication of the number of cattle required by the girl's family for her hand in marriage. Women make their own lip plates from locally dug clay, colour them with ochre and charcoal, and bake them in a fire.

After six months of stretching, the lip is so elastic that a plate can be slipped in and out without difficulty. The plates must always be worn in front of men and can only be taken out at private mealtimes, when sleeping, or in the presence of other women. In the past plates were wedge-shaped and made of balsa wood; more recently these have been replaced by round clay plates. Unlike lip plates, clay ear plugs are worn by both young girls and women for decoration alone.

SUCCEEDING PAGES (274 AND 275): In recent years, rifles have started to replace the traditional spear. These are used by the Surma in territorial disputes and cattle raids to protect themselves against their old enemies, the Bumi, who are themselves armed with more sophisticated automatic weapons.

(276 AND 277): Two Surma women, in private conversation, sport headdresses made from the skin of a wild cat.

Surma men paint their bodies in preparation for *donga* stick fights in order to emphasize their physical beauty and to intimidate their adversaries. They smear their bodies with a mixture of chalk and water and draw the designs with their fingertips, exposing the dark skin in a pattern of lines. The many varying designs are largely decorative and change daily.

Surma girls are painted by men, especially at the time of the *donga* stick fights.

OVERLEAF: Donga stick fights take place at the end of the rainy season and continue for a three-month period. Each week, chosen villages come together and the top fighters from each village challenge each other. Face painting and fierce looks (RIGHT) are intended to intimidate the opponent. The lethal iron wrist knife (LEFT) is an important weapon for the Surma and is used in cattle raids and territorial disputes. However, the carved wooden *donga* stick, with its distinctive phallic tip, is the only weapon used for stick fighting.

287

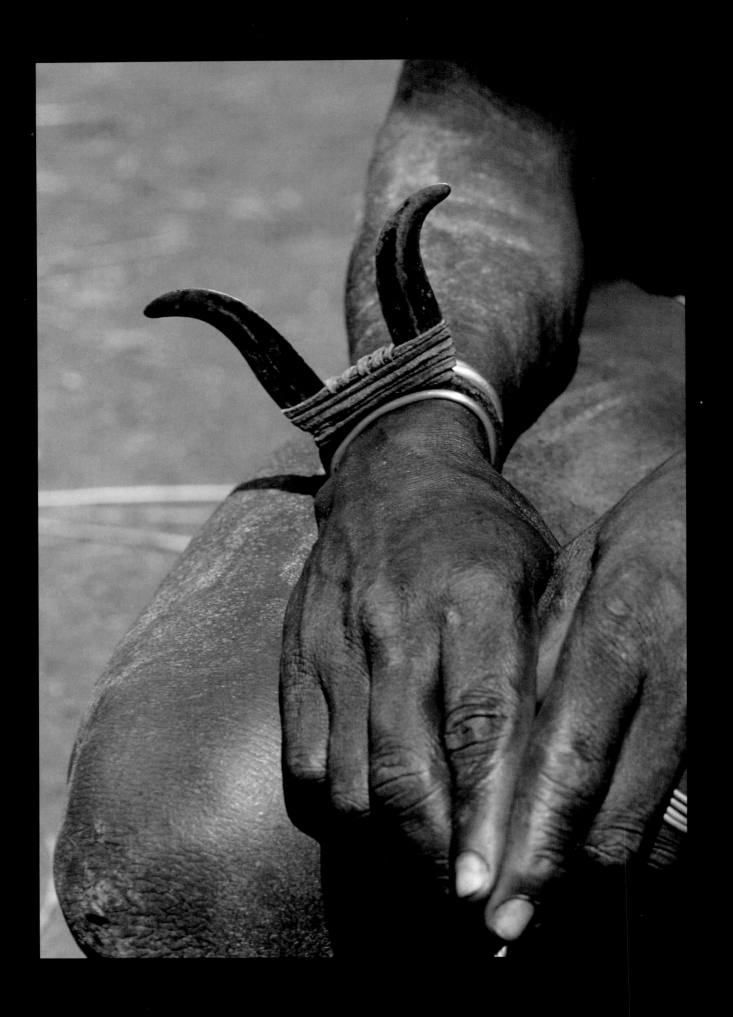

PRECEDING PAGES (290 AND 291): Groups of fighters holding their *donga* sticks high in the air, and chanting in frenzied rhythms, approach their opponents at the selected clearing in the forest where the fights will take place.

(292 AND 293): The most vulnerable parts of each fighter are meticulously bound in protective cotton wadding. Small hand and elbow shields made of tightly woven grass are also essential forms of protection.

ABOVE AND RIGHT: The stick fights are wild and fierce, for this is the time for men to prove their bravery in front of women. There are no rules to the game, short of killing one's opponent, which is absolutely prohibited. If a death does occur, the killer and his family are banished from the village.

OVERLEAF: Many fights occur in one day and the winners of each fight challenge one another until a victor emerges. He is then ceremonially lifted onto a platform of *donga* sticks and carried to a group of young women who wait at the edge of the fighting ground. One of these girls will choose the victor as her husband.

CHAPTER NINE

EPITAPH TO AN IDEA

The Karo of the Omo River

any of the tribes of the Lower Omo have shrunk in numbers to the point where their continued existence is now in doubt. Among these, the Karo – who live in just a few small villages along the banks of the Omo itself, and who number less than a thousand – seem the most threatened. A single epidemic could obliterate them. A single raid by a stronger group armed with automatic weapons could also wipe them out. But, in the end, it is the slow corrosion of the special "idea" they hold about themselves – the subversion of their culture by outside influences that is most likely to be their downfall.

Surprisingly in such a context – whether in their exuberant body painting, or in their dances and their celebrations – there continues to be something life-enhancing and life-affirming about this endangered group of people. Indeed, far from being over-shadowed by intimations of doom, they appear to enjoy moments of such happiness that the observer is briefly overtaken by a poignant sense of contact with something that mankind has long ago lost touch with elsewhere.

Bright-eyed and endlessly curious, the Karo have traditionally enjoyed a mode of existence as slow and unchanging as the wide and muddy river that meanders through their land. Somehow, though no Garden of Eden, their forgotten enclave remains a great-spirited place. Sadly, however, the Lower Omo cannot expect to preserve its splendid isolation much longer. Though it is only within the last decade that this region has collided to any extent with the wider world, the effects have already been shocking and, in many cases, irreversible.

Now touted as tourist attractions, encountering foreign sightseers for the first time, and facing the bleak prospect of "development" at the hands of governmental and foreign aid agencies, the Karo and their neighbours will soon be hard put to retain a single iota of their integrity. At best they seem destined to assimilation and the loss of their identity; at worst they confront the prospect of extinction. This is something that would be inconceivable in context of traditional society alone, however brutal that society may seem at times. The Karo, for instance, have a great deal in common with the much more numerous and more powerful Hamar. They speak virtually identical languages and they even graze their goats and cattle together on the same pastures. Custom allows the smaller group to survive alongside the larger one and to keep its identity intact. *Dembi*, the Hamar word for custom, is never interpreted or challenged by these related peoples – nor, for that matter, most of their neighbours. Custom allows them to order the chaos of the world – thus they do a thing because they have always done it, and they do it without questioning the way in which it is done or even why it is done at all. In fact, most of the isolated pastoralists, hunters and gatherers in this remote corner of southwest Ethiopia see custom and tradition as faultless constants. Rites of passage, age-grading systems, the ceremonies and styles of body decoration – all impose a wel-comed order and regularity on their lives.

Though they are aware of the forces encroaching upon them, the Karo still continue to honour the traditions of their ancestors with a verve that is truly breathtaking. These are the qualities that we have chosen to identify and portray in the pages of this final chapter which depicts the last days of a vanishing culture.

LEFT: Karo girl washing in the Omo river.   OVERLEAF: A Karo village of typical dome-shaped huts.

Before a celebration or dance, the Karo decorate their bodies with
a chalk paint, often imitating the spotted plumage of a guinea fowl.

Of all the Omo river peoples, the Karo excel in face and torso paintings. Elaborate face masks are created using locally found white chalk, yellow mineral rock, pulverized iron ore, and black charcoal.

PRECEDING PAGES (304 AND 305): Karo women scarify their chests to beautify themselves – it is said that the skin-texture of a scarified woman holds sensual appeal for men. The complete scarification of a man's chest indicates that he has killed an enemy or a dangerous animal. The scars are cut with a knife or razor blade and ash is rubbed in to produce a raised effect. The wearing of a grey and ochre clay hair bun also indicates the killing of an enemy or a dangerous animal. Both forms of decoration carry the same symbolic meaning for the Karo as they do for the Hamar.

At the end of the harvest and at times of initiation and marriage, the Karo come together to enjoy the seduction of dance. These dances often lead to marriage. A Karo man may take as many wives as he can afford, but usually he marries only two or three.

ABOVE, RIGHT AND SUCCEEDING PAGES (312 AND 313): As ochre, yellow and white paint transform the body, the spirit of the Karo is released. Ostrich feathers, which are worn as an indication of bravery, add the finishing touches to the overall effect.

(314 AND 315): Karo couples perform a rhythmic and pulsating dance, thrusting their hips one against the other in the dusty and frenetic atmosphere of early evening.

(316 AND 317): In long lines, men leap in unison towards the women, who come forward one by one to select the man of their choice.

(318 AND 319): Elders who are responsible for the wellbeing of the community hold a meeting in the cool shade of an acacia tree.

REFERENCES

PREFACE

1 For further details on the subject of past famines in Ethiopia, see the following: Graham Hancock, *Ethiopia: The Challenge of Hunger*, Gollancz, London, 1985; Richard Pankhurst, "The History of Famine and Pestilence in Ethiopia prior to the founding of Gondar", in *Journal of Ethiopian Studies*, Volume X, No.2, Addis Ababa, 1972; Richard Pankhurst, "The Great Ethiopian Famine of 1888–1892: A New Assessment", in *Journal of the History of Medicine*, Volume XXI, No.2, 1966.

INTRODUCTION

1 Ilmi Bowndheri, a Somali poet who allegedly died of love.

CHAPTER ONE

1 Rejecting the more familiar Gregorian system, Ethiopia still retains the Julian calendar, named after Julius Caesar – for whom it was devised by Alexandrian astronomers. The year is divided into twelve months of thirty days each and a thirteenth month of five or six days. Taking as its starting point the Birth of Christ – and owing to differences of opinion over the date of Creation – the Ethiopian calendar is seven years and eight months behind the Gregorian calendar.
2 See 2 Samuel 6.
3 See Edward Ullendorff, *Ethiopia and the Bible*, Oxford University Press (for the British Academy), 1968 (reprinted 1983 and 1988).

CHAPTER TWO

1 See Donald N. Levine, *Wax and Gold: Tradition and Innovation in Ethiopian Culture*, The University of Chicago Press, Chicago and London, 1965 (reprinted 1986).
2 David Kessler, *The Falashas: The Forgotten Jews of Ethiopia*, Shocken Books, New York, 1985.
3 Ibid.
4 Wolf Leslau, *A Falasha Anthology*, Yale University Press, 1951. See in particular the translation and elucidation of *Te-Ezaza Sanbat*, a Falasha literary work on the Commandments of the Sabbath.
5 David Buxton, *The Abyssinians*, Thames and Hudson, London, 1970.
6 A.M.M. Jones and E. Monroe, *A History of Ethiopia*, Oxford, 1960. These authors assert that it was only the fourth-century conversion to Christianity of the Axumite monarch Ezana – an accident of history – that "prevented Judaism from becoming the official religion of the Abyssinian kingdom".
7 Whether the Falashas are true Jews, or whether they are "Hebrao-Pagans" are matters that have been the subject of considerable controversy since at least the middle of the nineteenth century. Indeed it was not until 1973 that the Sephardi Chief Rabbi in Jerusalem ruled categorically in the Falashas' favour. Two years later the Ashkenazi Chief Rabbi followed suit, opening the way for the Israeli Ministry of the Interior to declare that the Falashas were indeed Jews and thus were entitled to automatic citizenship of Israel under the terms of the Law of Return.
8 Joseph Halevy, *La Guerre de Sarsa-Dengel contre les Falachas*, Paris, 1907.
9 See James Bruce, *Travels to Discover the Source of the Nile*, Edinburgh, 1790. Also Charles Tilstone Beke, writing in the *Jewish Chronicle*, London, 5 February 1847. And *The Falashas: The Jews of Ethiopia*, Minority Rights Group Report No. 67, London, July 1985.
10 For a full account of Operation Moses, see Minority Rights Group Report No. 67. op.cit. It is only fair to point out that the suffering of the Falashas during the 1984–85 famine was probably not a great deal worse than that of millions of their gentile compatriots who had no choice but to remain in appalling conditions in Ethiopia and in the refugee camps in the Sudan. As the Minority Rights Group observes: "The difference between the Falashas and the Christian and Muslim refugees from Ethiopia is simply that the Falashas had been offered a refuge elsewhere. The others had not." Particularly active in the nineteenth century.
   See Levine, op.cit.
   See Chapter One, Reference 1. With all the many saints' days and other observances taken into account, work is prohibited to the devout Ethiopian peasant for more than half the year.
14 See Chapter One, "Prayers of Stone", for an account.
15 Levine, op.cit.
16 *Encyclopaedia Britannica*.
17 Ullendorff, op.cit. To this day, the Nile springs are known as "Giyon".

CHAPTER THREE

1 S.F. Nesbit, *Desert and Forest*, London, 1934 (an account of a 1928 expedition in Afar country).
2 I.M. Lewis, *Peoples of the Horn of Africa: Somali, Afar and Saho*, International African Institute, London, 1955 (reprinted 1969).
3 J.S. Trimingham, *Islam in Ethiopia*, London, 1952.
4 A Hamitic people, closely related to the Afar and the Somali, the Oromo are the largest single ethnic group in the Horn: their numbers are estimated to exceed twenty million.
5 Quoted in D. Newbold, "The Beja Tribes of the Red Sea Hinterland", in J.A. Hamilton (Ed), *The Anglo-Egyptian Sudan from Within*, Faber and Faber, London, 1935.
6 Quoted by T.R.H. Owen, "The Hadendowa", in *Sudan Notes and Records*, Volume XX, No. 2, 1937.
7 Newbold, op.cit.
8 "The Manners, Customs and Beliefs of the Northern Beja", in *Sudan Notes and Records*, Volume XXI, No. 1, 1938.
9 H.A. MacMichael, *A History of the Arabs in the Sudan*, London, 1922.

CHAPTER FOUR

1 Andrew Paul, *A History of the Beja Tribes of the Sudan*, Oxford University Press, 1954.
2 Breasted, *Ancient Records of Egypt*, quoted in Andrew Paul, op.cit.
3 *Somalia in Word and Image*, Foundation for Cross-Cultural Understanding, Indiana University Press, 1986.
4 Ibid.
5 John Eames, *The Beauty of the Kenya Coast*, Westland Sundries Ltd., Nairobi, 1986.
6 *Somalia in Word and Image*, op.cit.
7 H.A.R. Gibb (Ed), *The Travels of Ibn Battuta AD 1325–1354*, Cambridge University Press, 1962.
8 Cited in *Somalia in Word and Image*, op.cit.
9 J.S. Trimingham, *Islam in Ethiopia*, Oxford University Press, 1952.
10 Lt. Cruttenden, *Memoir on the Western or Odoor Tribes inhabiting the Somali Coast of N.E. Africa*, London, 1848. His account of the atmosphere of the Berbera fair, which he describes as "a perfect Babel, in confusion as in languages", is worthy of repetition. "No chief is acknowledged," he records. "Disputes between the inland tribes daily arise and are settled by the spear and the dagger, the combatants retiring to the beach at a short distance from the town in order that they may not disturb the trade. Long strings of camels are arriving and departing day and night, escorted generally by women alone, until at a distance from the town; and an occasional group of dusky and travel-worn children marks the arrival of the slave Cafila from Hurrur and Efat."
11 Ibid.
12 Capt. Sir Richard F. Burton, *First Footsteps in East Africa*, Darf Publishers, London, 1986 (first published 1856).
13 *Rimbaud: Complete Works, Selected Letters*, University of Chicago Press, Chicago and London, 1966.
14 This story, recorded in discussion with Brava residents, is strikingly reminiscent of a similar tale in British tradition which has it that, in the Dark Ages, the Danes acquired land in southern England by using an identical "ox-skin" trick.

CHAPTER FIVE

1 Capt. Sir Richard F. Burton, *First Footsteps in East Africa*, Darf Publishers, London, 1986. First published 1856.
2 I.M. Lewis, the leading anthropologist in this field, tells a revealing story of his own stay in a Somali camel camp: "In extreme drought and heat few camels were in milk and the camel boys were living just at subsistence level with no water to alleviate their thirst. One morning a young camel-herd came to my tent to beg water, not, as he emphasised, for himself, but for two young camels which were sorely in need . . ." I.M. Lewis, op.cit.
3 The Ogaden are a powerful section of the great Darod clan-family.
4 Burton, op.cit.
5 B.W. Andrzejewski, *Hikmad Soomaali*, Oxford University Press, 1956.
6 From a poem by Hassan Sheikh Mumin in *Somalia in Word and Image*, Foundation for Cross-Cultural Understanding, Indiana University Press, 1986.
7 Excerpt from a poem by Mahamud Tukaale in *Somalia in Word and Image*, op.cit.
8 Burton, op.cit. This British adventurer, a notorious philanderer, was much attracted to Somali women and described them as preferring "amourettes with strangers, following the well-known Arab proverb, 'the newcomer filleth the eye'".
9 Excerpt from a poem by Hassan Sheikh Mumin in *Somalia in Word and Image*, op.cit.

CHAPTER SIX

1 Lambert Bartels, *Oromo Religion: Myths and Rites of the Western Oromo of Ethiopia – An Attempt to Understand*, Dietrich Reimer Verlag, Berlin, 1983.
2 Ibid.
3 Donald N. Levine, *Greater Ethiopia: The Evolution of a Multi-Ethnic Society*, University of Chicago Press, Chicago and London, 1974.
4 G.W.B. Huntingford, *The Galla of Ethiopia*, International African Institute, London, 1952.
5 Ibid.
6 C.G. Seligman, *Races of Africa*, Oxford University Press, 1966.
7 Huntingford, op.cit.
8 See L. Randall Powels, *Horn and Crescent: Cultural Change and Traditional Islam on the East African Coast, 800–1900*, Cambridge University Press, 1987.

CHAPTER SEVEN

1 Miressa Gamtessa, an elder of the Matcha Oromo, quoted in Lambert Bartels, *Oromo Religion: Myths and Rites of the Western Oromo of Ethiopia – An Attempt to Understand*, Dietrich Reimer Verlag, Berlin, 1983.
2 C.F. Buckingham and G.W.B. Huntingford, *Some Records of Ethiopia 1593–1646*, The Hakluyt Society, 1954.
3 P.T.W. Baxter, "Boran Age-Sets and Warfare", in Fukui Katsuyoshi and David Turton (Eds), *Warfare Amongst East African Herders*, National Museum of Ethnology, Osaka, 1977.
4 G.W.B. Huntingford, *The Galla of Ethiopia*, International African Institute, London, 1952.
5 Baxter, op.cit. See also Chapter Six, "Spirit Worlds", for an account of the *gada* system which was, originally, a pan-Oromo institution but is today largely confined to the Borana.
6 The quotation is from Samuel Johnson, *The History of Rasselas, Prince of Abyssinia*, Penguin, London, 1976 (first published 1759). Johnson, of course, knew nothing of the Borana; however his description of a fictional Bedouin tribe fits them well.
7 C.R. Hallpike, *The Konso of Ethiopia: A Study of the Values of a Cushitic People*, Clarendon Press, Oxford, 1972. Note the similarity of this practice to that of the Afar with their *das* memorials – see Chapter 3, "The Desert at the Mountains' Feet".
8 Baxter, op.cit. The Konso use the word *lallasha* rather than *kallaacha*.
9 Hallpike, op.cit.
10 Ibid.

CHAPTER EIGHT

1 Ernesta Cerulli, *Peoples of South-West Ethiopia and its Borderland*, International African Institute, London, 1956. See also Tesfaye Lemma, *Ethiopian Musical Instruments*, Addis Ababa, 1975. See also Peter George Murdock, *Africa: Its Peoples and Their Cultural History*, McGraw-Hill Book Company, 1959.
2 David Turton, "War, Peace and Mursi Identity", in Katsuyoshi and Turton, op.cit.
3 Serge Tornay, "Armed Conflict in the Lower Omo Valley", in Katsuyoshi and Turton, op.cit.